# Why Not Me?

Toni Noel

Published by M P Publishing, S. D., 2024.

While every precaution has been taken in the preparation of this book, the publisher assumes no responsibility for errors or omissions, or for damages resulting from the use of the information contained herein.

WHY NOT ME?

**First edition. December 10, 2024.**

Copyright © 2024 Toni Noel.

ISBN: 979-8230297390

Written by Toni Noel.

# Table of Contents

This book is dedicated to all my children, grand-children and great-grandchildren.You know who you are.

Memoir

# Chapter One

Planting the Seed

As I sat in my mother's lap and waited for my siblings to walk the three miles home from school, Momma would turn the pages of my baby book and share stories about our family. Those stories stuck with me and became so familiar it seems as if I were present for all the events related here, not for just some of them.

Momma taught me the love of books, and out of the stories she read to me and told, grew my desire to write.

In tenth grade, I wrote a short autobiography. Short because I'd discovered I hadn't accomplished enough notable things to fill a book. To make my story more interested I ended mine after the fourth chapter, when I gave myself a fatal disease and killed me off.

I kept those thoughts to myself, but set out to prove the speaker wrong, so it's little wonder that before I'd even learned to read, a college education became my goal. Perhaps because my parents insisted college was beyond their means. Their roots did not go deep. Thanks to the deepening Great Depression, the bank repossessed the first home Daddy built for his growing family and they'd moved us four times because of the depression.

With four little mouths he had to feed, so my ultimate goal – me acquiring a college degree was the least of his worries. One of my earliest memories is of constantly being told, "There's no way under the sun you can ever do that," and me thinking to myself, *Why not me?*

I've always loved the story of how my parents met.

In the 1920's, my grandparents, William and Rosa Mae Bailey, ran a high-class dance hall in downtown Birmingham, Alabama, a dime-a-dance place where lonely men came to dance with pretty girls beneath a rotating mirrored ball, and it's where my parents met.

William's other daughters worked there, too, dancing with any man with enough money in his pocket to pay for a dance. Like the other women working there, Annie Laura and Edith Bailey were only allowed to dance twice in a night with the same man. There, under the watchful eyes of her parents, Annie Laura met and fell in love with the man she would soon marry.

Laura, as our closest relatives called her, longed to escape her dull life, while Robert was tired of hopping freight trains, and dodging rail yard guards. He wanted to settle down and took his first step in that direction that evening when he garnered Will's permission to dance with Laura, then bought all her dance tickets for the rest of the night.

Before coming to the dance hall Laura had heated a curling iron over a kerosene lamp and curled her thick, long brown hair so that it hung in ringlets about her face. Robert seemed unable to take his eyes off her, Edith recalled. "He looked so handsome in his brown serge suit every young woman there fell a little in love with him that night. I watched with envy as he moved Laura across the floor like Fred Astaire did when he stepped out in a smooth fox trot. Robert literally swept Laura off her feet."

"Love at first sight," Daddy proudly confided when asked about meeting seventeen-year-old Annie Laura while he waited to leave town later that night by hopping the next west bound freight.

She'd always wanted to travel, and when her handsome dance partner, a twenty-eight-year-old magazine salesman, told her he'd "sold magazines in every state in the Union but two," Robert stole her heart.

In just a matter of hours the two of them were head over heels in love. Later that night Robert hopped a freight that would eventually take him to St. Louis, where Robert had pledged to sell magazines for a while, then come dance with Annie Laura again. After a few weeks in St. Louis, Robert quit his job to hurry back to Laura, and caught a slow-moving freight for a reunion with the beautiful young woman who'd promised to wait for him.

When school started, Laura would have been a high school senior but, aware her parents couldn't afford to buy her a graduation dress, she married Robert on September 19, 1925, instead of finishing school.

She always regretted not having that diploma, but she wouldn't reveal those regrets for many years. She feared her long-time friends she'd made since her marriage might discover she'd fooled them all those years. This worry kept her from going back to school to earn her high school diploma, but when her children came along she allowed nothing to keep them from attending school.

After their wedding, Laura and Robert rented a little house in Fountain Heights, a North Birmingham suburb. Laura kept house. Robert had learned carpentry from his father, but soon became apprenticed to an electrician, which meant joining the electrical union and paying weekly Union dues.

Where there were unions there were strikes, most often for better working conditions, less often for more pay, but in hard times the union paid benefits. A firm supporter of the Union, my father steadfastly refused to ever cross a picket line.

Even in the best of times construction work came to a halt in Birmingham around Thanksgiving when the weather turned cold and wouldn't pick up again until the spring thaw. Electricians couldn't string wire in freezing weather and even inside jobs halted until Spring. Most union leaders spread around what little work there was, making sure each of its members put in a few hours a week, which would guarantee enough money in each pay envelope to cover their weekly union dues, but often little else.

Robert didn't dare miss work to stay home with Laura and wait for the birth of their first child, so when Laura went into labor on July 21, 1926, an unemployed friend drove her to the hospital for the birth of a son they named Robert Huewell Page, Junior, but decided to call their baby Little Robert to distinguish father and son. A sturdy baby with inquisitive blue eyes, he kept his parents on their toes.

Sixteen months later, Juanita Marilyn Page joined the family. When she finally learned to walk, the shy but single-minded toddler trailed after her brother on most of his harrowing escapades.

As the depression deepened, making work even more scarce, Mr. Norwood, owner of the electrical shop where Big Robert worked, paid him out of his own pocket to remodel the Norwoods' house. At the same time, Robert was building his family a four- room bungalow on property he'd bought from friends.

He moved his growing family into their new home in early March of 1929, just before the birth of Annie Laura's namesake, a feisty, olive skinned daughter with Laura's dark hair and shiny brown eyes. The tiny baby came down with whooping cough soon after her birth and nearly died.

Ann, as her sister and brother called her, turned three about the time the bank foreclosed on their home. With no place to live, no work and little food for their table, Laura and Robert wrote to his family in Georgia for help. His relatives couldn't send money, but invited the young family to come live with them. Robert left his Model-T with a friend – since the banks crashed, no one could afford to drive a car—and loaded his family onto an excursion train headed for Columbus, Georgia, where his mother, two brothers and five sisters lived.

The women, all skilled dressmakers, took in sewing to supplement the family income. Laura, also a talented seamstress, pitched in to do her share.

All the Georgia cousins were towheads. My sisters, one with brown eyes, and both with darker hair, were ostracized by their blond-headed cousins. Only fair-skinned Little Robert looked as if he belonged, I'm told.

The female cousins had to share their bed with their poorer cousins and never forgave their unfortunate relatives from Birmingham for invading their home. When tempers flared because of the overcrowding, Robert took his family back to Alabama for a while.

When work ran out he'd take his family back to Georgia to endure more insults.

Laura could never abide nicknames. Only her side of the family was allowed to call her Laura. She insisted the Georgia relatives use her full name, which to them seemed like their brother's wife was putting on unnecessary airs.

She helped with the cooking and sewing and bit her tongue when her sisters-in-law criticized her efforts, which they often did. Only her mother-in-law understood her plight and defended her.

Then a bout of morning sickness caused the sisters to gang up on Momma.

"Don't you know how to stop having babies?" one asked.

"Our brother doesn't need another mouth to feed.."

Laura packed up her family and Robert took them home.

Back in Birmingham, with the depression deepening, disheartened unemployed men openly wept in the street. Others called, "Lady, can you spare a dime?" when Laura walked by with her brood, something I doubt those men ever dreamed of having to do.

Industrious men sold pencils or apples on the street corner. The hardest hit ones committed suicide.

Until she was too burdened by the coming infant to make the trip Laura and her little ones rode the streetcar to town and stood in bread lines so they'd have something to eat each day.

Requests for Union benefits continued to exceed the Union's income from dues, and its leaders struggled to keep the Union afloat. Laura and Robert let other bills ride to pay those Union dues. They didn't dare miss a week. If his dues were in arrears, his membership in the Union would lapse, and Robert's name would no longer appear on the list of members actively seeking work. He'd lose all chance of getting hired and all rights to future benefits.

Sometimes a man would stop by the Union Hall offering to hire an electrician for a good day's work. If Robert was there at the time and lucky, he'd get hired, so he did a lot of hanging-out at the Union Hall, protecting his right to work. He'd learned a family man had to stand up for himself, and work hard when he did get hired.

He spent some of his hanging-out time in prayer, I imagine, wondering if God had deserted his family. While men in other cities were finding regular work, unemployment still ran deep in Birmingham. Soup kitchens occupied downtown street corners and Robert only left the Union Hall long enough to stand in line for one hot meal a day, so Laura could stretch the meager supply of food in her pantry for one more day.

By my birth in late August of 1933, Daddy had exhausted every legal means of keeping food on the table for his growing family. Only his God-given strength, the kindness of those more fortunate and a poor man's pride kept his family together in their small rented house.

Since Birmingham summers are hot and humid August is not the ideal month to give birth. It goes without saying Momma was delighted to welcome me into the world at the Norwood Hospital that sticky morning. Daddy still couldn't afford gas for his car, so friends drove us home from the hospital.

One man helped Momma up the front steps and into the house while the other one carried me indoors. As the friends were leaving, those same steps they'd just carried me up gave way beneath their feet. No one was seriously hurt. In retelling those events, Momma always thanked the good Lord that those steps had held up until we'd safely made it inside.

That was the house with the porch swing where Momma nursed me, the same porch swing that fell with us one afternoon.

A baby born in the depression continued to nurse for as long as the mother produced milk, a dependable source of nourishment during hard times. So for the first two years of my life, I received six meals a day from my mother's soft, warm breast. Even after I'd cut a full mouthful of teeth I eagerly latched onto her nipple while she kept the depression at bay for me with her stories and songs.

"The first words you ever spoke formed a complete sentence," Momma proudly told me. "You were always a big tease and took great pleasure in biting my nipple."

This had caused her to often threaten, "'I'll whippie you,'" in hopes of distracting me from clamping down hard.

"One day," she said, "you reared back your little blonde head and with a big grin said your first words. "'I'll pippie uu,'"

As we rocked together in that porch swing, Momma entertained me with stories about Little Robert, the bane of her existence though she dearly loved her first born. From the minute he learned to walk, my brother found ways to run away.

For his second birthday Momma and Daddy gave him a little red wagon. He pulled it everywhere. One morning, he woke up early and slipped out of the house before dawn. Trailing his wagon, the little dickens took off down the street.

Momma's milkman recognized the little boy dragging a red wagon several blocks away, hurrying down the sidewalk on short, chubby legs. The milkman stopped his truck and offered the runaway a ride.

The thoughtful delivery man stuffed the red wagon in the back of his truck with his bottles of milk, stood Little Robert between his legs and drove him home. Awakened by the milkman's knock, my parents were stunned to discover their son had quietly unlocked the front door and escaped without a sound.

Daddy moved the locks higher. It didn't help. For the better part of a week Robert shoved a chair over, climbed up on it and unlocked each new device Daddy installed, earning his freedom more times than Momma liked to count.

A hook fastened on the outside of the toddler's bedroom door finally kept him safely inside while they slept. The little boy's wanderlust failed to diminish, even after he grew up. Except for Daddy's constantly tanning of Little Robert's hide with a belt, and Momma sadly shaking her head with chagrin each time she told me about his misdeeds, I don't remember much about those times.

# Chapter Two

1934-1936

Valley View

My earliest recollections are of Valley View, and what I considered the idyllic life we lived there. I was completely unaware we were poor. By the time I realized it, my family was shedding the last remnants of poverty and getting back on their feet.

My parents always kept the wolf from the door, made sure we four children had the necessities of life, nourishing food, new shoes for the start of school, and a pre-owned, gently-worn, warm coat to wear once the weather turned cold.

So, what if the sleeves of Juanita's coat are a little short on her long arms? Her rapid growth should slow down soon. No sense buying another coat this late in the school year," Momma would say, and I had no way of knowing she was unable to buy her a new coat right then, even though wearing the outgrown coat embarrassed Juanita to tears.

In 1934 a row of old wooden houses originally built for coal miners became available for two dollars a month rent. William Bailey and the families of his son and two daughters quickly moved in.

There, we were allowed to have pets, probably more than we could afford to feed, but the warm fur of a loving animal went a long way towards making a child forget its hunger, surrounded by unconditional love, and our house in Valley View abounded with love.

And books. I have no idea where they came from. I don't remember seeing a bookcase in our relatives' homes, but Momma read to us from a book every day. It was at her knee I developed my love for the printed word. At bedtime she'd mark the page she left off reading from Little Women or The Five Little Peppers and How They Grew, and before she tucked us in the following night, she'd sit on our bed and we'd silently listen to her read the next chapter or two.

"I'm too old," Little Robert argued, "to share story hour," but I could see him seated on the sofa idly turning the pages of Tom Sawyer or one of his *Big-Little Books*, his head cocked toward our room, while the words Momma read spun fantasies in our heads.

She read with such expression we cried over Beth Marsh's death, laughed with Tom Thumb and sang for our supper when asked.

Every afternoon I had my own private story time on our front porch. No matter how busy she was, when it came time for her older children to come home from school, Momma would take the old nursery rhyme book with missing pages out to the porch swing and read to me. Not in the same swing that fell with us. This one was sturdy and new and made just for our porch during Daddy's father's visit the year before. My Grandpa Page.

The depression took its toll on your Daddy," Momma told me one day with tears in her eyes when I asked. "It crushed his pride, forced him to accept day labor. Your Father has never been afraid of hard work, and would take any job offered him. Money earned from a few hours of digging ditches sometimes fed our family for a week."

Some mornings he'd follow the streetcar line over the mountain into Birmingham, picking up discarded soft drink bottles along the way, she told me. He'd redeem the bottles, spend his windfall on as much day-old bread as he could carry, then hike back home, a tired but grateful man. And for the next few days our family would have toast with our oatmeal.

While work was scarce Daddy raised chickens, goats, hogs and cows in pens on the hill behind our house. He turned the earth in an unfenced plot of ground above the outhouse with a shovel and carefully pressed corn and bean seeds into the rich soil. When the vegetables matured, all the relatives helped Momma can green beans, tomatoes, and soup mix, which all the families shared.

In Daddy's spare time, he made a rope swing, a see-saw, and a spinning Jennie for us from other people's discards. The best thing was the playhouse he built for us beneath the limbs of the huge chinaberry tree growing in the side yard. Constructed of sturdy skinned logs, the playhouse was the envy of all our cousins and friends. Waist-high walls and a roof set on tall poles let in the sunshine and cooling breezes, but kept out the rain.

We furnished it with the child size settee and chair Grandpa Page made for us. This miniaturized set was identical to the wooden furniture he'd made for our parents to sit on while they shelled butter beans on the porch. He was a skilled carpenter, but when he couldn't find work, he drank. When his drinking got bad, the Georgia relatives sent him to visit us.

My two sisters and I fought over the doll bed he made us. Three little girls and just one bed for our dolls – surely he knew only one bed would cause problems. We had lots of hand-me-down dolls from Georgia. Shirley Temples dolls with corkscrew curls. Baby dolls with fancy dresses fashioned from scraps of material left over from our own clothes, clothes Momma stitched by hand late at night for Christmas gifts. Momma Rosie, my girlish-looking grandmother, made the rest, and all through the long humid summers we kept the dirt floor of the doll house swept and took care of our dolls and pets.

Valley View was a great place to raise animals, whether livestock or pets. I remember the chickens, hogs and goats best. Twice a day Daddy milked the cow. I'd wait for him to finish, then follow him into the kitchen with the brimming bucket of rich, warm milk. To this day, I miss drinking warm milk straight from the cow.

Now, I prefer my milk cold.

I named one of our dogs Portia, after Momma's favorite soap opera, "Portia Faces Life," which she and I listened to while everyone else was at school. Daddy complained that our dog was regularly dropping litters of unwanted pups but, awed by the miracle of birth, I didn't agree.

It amazed me that one day there would be just one dog, the next day, a box full of squirming, whimpering puppies that needed me to help them nurse.

Where had they all come from?

Watching those tiny bundles grow became a favorite pastime. Warm, already fat, and always blind when born, the tiny pups constantly lost their grip on Portia's nipples, and needed me to hook them up again. Portia, like the service station hose that magically filled the gas tank of Daddy's car whenever it showed empty, had to fill six empty tummies several times a day.

Her babies grew fast, pretty soon opening their eyes and no longer needing my help. Soon after, Portia would start weaning her litter by constantly trotting around the yard, refusing to lie down and nurse. The bravest and most determined puppy would latch onto a dinner bottle and dangle there until Portia snapped at the puppy and it fell off in the dirt, my first introduction to the harsh reality of life.

Somehow we always found good homes for those puppies among our relatives and neighbors there on the hill, where pets roamed free and were accidentally run over with heartbreaking frequency.

Portia's life came to a sudden end, a mange cure gone terribly wrong. In a house where children seldom saw a doctor, taking a pet to the Vet was out of the question. Besides, home remedies usually worked best on mange, the scourge of a poor family's dogs.

Somebody told Daddy to rub the infected area with creosote, which he happened to have. Since Portia was pretty much covered with dry, itchy scales and had lost most of her hair, he thought a creosote dip would work better and gave it a try. Portia died the following day.

Daddy had already buried her when I found out she'd died. I cried anyway. Next day he brought home a new puppy a man on his job claimed needed a new home.

After the depression eased and Daddy found steady work, he began driving his Model-T to work. Every afternoon the dogs would set up a clamor when they heard his car leave the pavement and start bumping over the rutted gravel road on the way home, not quieting until he pulled into our yard.

The dogs' enthusiastic barking reminded Momma to pull the coffee pot onto the hottest part of the wood stove. Daddy's love of coffee was legend and we were all in trouble if the fire went out and let the pot get cold. He expected to smell the coffee perking when he came in the door.

Remembering Daddy's Model-T brings back painful memories. One weekend when I was three, one of his tires went flat. He and Little Robert took off the tire, pulled out the inner tube, and carried it off to the workshop in back to patch it, leaving the shiny tireless wheel standing on its rim in the drive.

It looked like a new toy and I circled it once or twice, then moved in closer and accidentally bumped into it. The heavy wheel tipped over. The rim landed on my bare big toe. To this day I still recall the pain, and the speed with which my injured toenail turned black.

To help Daddy make money, Momma sold her extra eggs and goat's milk to little, dark-skinned boys I wasn't allowed to play with who came twice a week to buy eggs. The boys were scared of our goats, especially Bad Bob. He tried to eat everything in sight, especially the faded pants and shirts those little boys wore.

Whenever the dogs commenced to barking in the middle of the day we'd all rush outside and hear the boys yelling, "Miz Page, come get your goat."

For a while we had a dog that killed chickens, not a good thing when we depended on those chickens for our livelihood. Daddy tried everything to break the dog of that habit, even tied a dead chicken around his neck. It didn't work, it just stunk. We had to get rid of the dog. A hen house and a chicken eating dog couldn't survive in our neighborhood.

At some point, the years in Valley View start to run together, but I remember clearly my morning routine. Momma Rosa lived right across the road from us and with Momma's permission, as soon as my siblings left for school, I'd run over to her house for my daily visit. She'd feed me country biscuits smothered in butter and strong black coffee whitened with thick cream while I sat at a little table behind my Grandmother's big, black, wood-burning cook stove.

Weekdays, my grandpa, Papa Will, drove an ambulance. On weekends, he led his own band. I've forgotten what instrument he played. On warm nights all the relatives would gather on someone's porch and talk about their day and the days to come while watching the children play Red Rover and Kick the Can until it grew too dark.

Sometimes they'd sing, but the evening always ended with Uncle Ralph murmuring, "Times have got to get better, or what's a honest man to do?"

None of the lapped-wood siding on the houses in Valley View had seen a coat of paint. Our house sat way up off the ground in front, had five rooms and wooden floors hidden beneath linoleum rugs. Daddy rigged a pipe to bring cold running water from the backyard well to the kitchen sink when anybody pumped.

Kerosene lamps provided light. A big one hung from a pulley mounted on the ceiling right above the table where we ate. After dinner my sisters would lower the lamp and sit on Daddy-built benches pulled up to both sides of the table and do their homework.

One night the last one up forgot to turn down the lamp when they went to bed. The wick burned down too low. Next morning, we discovered soot had blackened the once-white ceilings and walls and Daddy had to repaint every room.

One evening after instructing my older sisters and brother to keep the fire going in the kitchen stove, my parents went out. Sometime later, my siblings remembered the fire and sent me to check on it.

Not a hint of warmth came from the stove. My sisters would get into real trouble for playing checkers with me and having such a good time they'd forgotten to keep an eye on the stove. *How hard could it be to restart a fire?* I wondered, pouring kerosene over what I thought were cold embers the way I had seen Daddy do.

The instant the oil dribbled over the cooling embers, hot flames shot up in my face with a loud noise. Frightened by the explosion, I shut my eyes and didn't open them until my sisters started shouting at me. Ashes and bits of something black rained down around me.

"Your beautiful white hair," Juanita mourned.

"Momma is going to kill us," Annie Laura wailed.

The pungent odor of burned hair hung in the house. A ring of black circled my face. A quick glance in Daddy's shaving mirror that hung by the stove revealed stubby, blackened eyebrows above my stunned blue eyes.

Unbelieving, I reached up to touch my hair. Where soft curls had recently bounced against my rosy cheeks, a strange stiffness met my fingertips. Those black bits still drifting down from the ceiling were the ashes of my singed hair!

When my parents came home my sisters received a stern scolding for sending a child to do their job. "It's a wonder my precious baby wasn't scarred for life," I heard Momma say.

Being the baby had certain privileges. While my siblings went to school, I got to stay home with Momma. Some days we'd walk through the woods to Homewood, catch the streetcar that ran over the hill past Vulcan, made a sharp turn onto Twentieth Street and continued past Five Points into downtown Birmingham. I liked to shop with Momma, even when she didn't buy and only went to town to pay a little on her layaways. For the longest there wasn't much she could afford to buy, but I didn't know that, and didn't miss what I'd never had.

In the winter when construction closed down and Daddy was without work, we ate a lot of oatmeal, and big, flat, dried butter beans.

Prior to each meal, we girls set the table with the pale green dishes that came free in boxes of oatmeal. Momma could stretch the tiniest piece of beef, heaps of potatoes and onions into a delicious stew everybody liked.

Sometimes we received packages from Georgia in the mail. Daddy's family sent at least one box of used clothing every year. When they sent money, it came in an envelope, but the things I liked to receive best were the new clothes Grandmother Jeannie made for me. I was so small she could make things for me from leftover scraps. Daddy later proudly claimed I inherited my love of sewing from her.

Although she always managed to have work, either as a licensed practical nurse or a seamstress in a sweatshop, Momma Rosie also found time to sew for me.

Momma made a lot of our dresses on an old treadle sewing machine. She also turned hems and remade dresses she passed down to the next one of us in line.

For years, Momma didn't attend church with us because she didn't have a Sunday dress, I later learned, but she made certain we each had one good outfit for church. After the service Daddy would hurry us home for lunch. While Momma got it on the table he'd tell her about my Sunday School teacher pulling up my dress and calling the other teachers' attention to the lace Momma had hand-stitched on my underpants. I think his tales kept her from feeling bad because she couldn't go to church with me.

She relied on sales at Kress's and Woolworth's for new clothes for her growing girls. Each spring at the six-for-five-dollars sale she'd choose six dresses each for Juanita and Ann, put them in layaway and pay thirty-five cents a week all summer so that in the Fall, they both had new dresses for school. The fall I started to school, she brought home six dresses from layaway for me, too.

The dresses I admired most of my sisters had tucked bodices of striped flowers and pleated skirts. On the skirts the strips of flowers alternated with solid strips, pink and brown on Ann's, pink and green on Juanita's, and I couldn't wait until I grew into them.

Every item of wearable clothing passed down to the next child in line. By the time those dresses reached me the colors had faded to muddy brown and a sick green. I didn't mind. Growing into something that had been my sisters was irrefutable proof I was getting bigger, even if the scales didn't agree.

I eventually grew into Juanita's clothes, although her dresses never looked right on me. Now I know the reason. Momma chose bright fall colors for Juanita and muted pastel colors for Ann. Considering their coloring, those choices should have been reversed. Juanita and I share similar coloring, and fall colors make me look sick.

Until he landed a job and moved away, Uncle William Bailey, Momma's brother, lived with his wife Jo and their two sons in a house down the hill from Momma Rosie's. Before they married, Aunt Jo lived in Norwood not far from where my parents lived. When Uncle William stayed too late visiting her and missed the last street car he'd show up on Momma's doorstep late at night, knowing she'd take him in, even though she did not have a spare bed.

He shared Momma and Daddy's bed. They were slight of build, Uncle William was not, and on those nights, they found themselves crowded out of their own bed.

Momma's youngest sister Jeanette and her husband Ralph moved into Uncle William's rental house when he and Aunt Jo moved to Bessemer from Valley View. The new residents were so near our own age we were not required to call them aunt and uncle. In fact, Jeanette was not much older than Ann. The two of them became close friends, a fact that bothered Momma, who feared Ann was passing gossip from our house to theirs.

Across the road from us, on the other side of Momma Rosie's, Aunt Edith and Uncle Bernie Durham lived with their two children, Freddie and Diane, the cousins nearest my age, Freddie being a year older, Diane two years younger. I liked them best, and on Sundays they rode to church with us.

One day the three of us were playing "gotcha" around and behind their living room sofa. Freddie reached for Diane over the back, and when she playfully pulled his arm, it broke. Even though it was all in fun, Aunt Edith scolded us something fierce, because his hurt arm required a visit to the doctor and he came home with his arm in a cast, I supposed.

Not long after that Freddie was hospitalized. One of my earliest recollections is of overhearing my folks discussing his illness. From their hushed whispers I knew they thought something bad was going to happen to him, I just didn't know what.

He was a pretty little boy. The Durhams and the Pages who live in Georgia all have white-white hair and sparkling blue eyes. Freddie had them, too, and these traits gave Freddie an angelic look. Born with serious health problems, he'd been sickly most of his life. Cancer of the kidney, it turned out.

Every time he went back to the hospital for radiation therapy—something else my parents whispered about – they'd go visit him. We'd spend Sunday afternoon waiting for them in our car in the hospital's parking lot, Ann thumbing through well-worn movie magazines, Robert engrossed in a Dick Tracey comic book, Juanita wiggling from boredom, and me wondering why I wasn't allowed into the hospital to visit Freddie, my best friend.

I hated those visits. I somehow knew from the tears in Momma's eyes when she came back to the car that Freddie was never coming home.

I don't remember his funeral, other than there was a lot of white around him—his casket, the pretty suit he wore, and the flowers covering his small grave.

Diane had pretty blonde curls, but after Freddie's death, instead of showering her with love, Aunt Edith and Uncle Bernie acted as though they resented the fact she'd survived instead of him.

The loss of her brother saddened Diane, but only being three-years-old, she didn't know how to grieve. Worse still, she felt unloved. "It's like nothing I ever do is right," she later told me, making my heart ache for her.

I was lucky. We might not have had much, but I never once questioned my parents' love.

It seemed folks we knew were always dying. I recall standing by a lot of open graves while the people I loved most wept.

Then one night an ambulance took Papa Will away and I never saw him alive again. Most of us didn't have a chance to say goodbye until we stood by his open grave. He died in the hospital of a ruptured heart, some whispered, but Momma said, "No. Papa was taken from us too soon because an aneurism ruptured in his lung."

I decided to stay away from hospitals because all the folks I knew who went there to get better left in a hearse.

# Chapter Three

1936

The First Christmas I Remember

My parents were hard hit by the Great Depression and often struggled to make the Christmas Holidays a happy time for us.

One year my grandmother gave Daddy a subscription to the *Saturday Evening Post*, and kept renewing the subscription until the publisher couldn't keep up with changing times and stopped publishing it. Daddy had always read everything he could get his hands on, and now he had something of his own. We were not allowed to touch the newest issue until Daddy said we could.

We all loved that magazine, and would gather around each time the mailman brought a new issue to see what Norman Rockwell had put on the cover that week. Next morning Daddy would carry his newest magazine out to the outhouse, and stay for a really long time. I didn't much like to spend any more time than necessary out there, but apparently he did. I think it was because it was the only place he could go and not be surrounded by females.

The Christmas morning of 1936 is the first holiday to stay in my memory. I woke to the soft strains of a lullaby coming from beneath our tree and to the cheers of my siblings who were delighted I'd finally opened my eyes so they could get up.

Momma said, "Wake up, Sugar. Santa Claus came," and I hurried into the living room. Beneath the sagging branches of the tree we'd cut and dragged down off the hill I discovered the source of the music, a baby doll nestled in her own carrying case. The noise and excitement of those around me opening their gifts failed to draw my attention away from my perfect doll.

When I picked her up, her brown eyes opened, I snuggled her soft body close, and when I laid her back in bed, she slowly closed her eyes, a smile on her face as she enjoyed the tinkling strains from the music box.

To this day I have a fascination with music boxes, and still have that one. I can't recall what anyone else received for Christmas, or even if I received other gifts. My doll earned my full attention from the moment I first laid eyes on her. I fell hopelessly in love with her and named her Priscilla.

She was just the right size to fit in a towheaded four-year-old child's arms. Rocking her, I would not have to hold her long before the music lulled her to sleep.. Then I'd put her down in her own little bed.

The latch on the lid was to secure her for traveling, but I didn't like locking the lid down right in her face and never latched it with Priscilla inside. Of all the dolls I ever owned, she was my favorite. She had a cry box hidden in her soft rounded chest but a good mother didn't let her baby cry. Priscilla wore panties instead of diapers, but came with a bottle I soon wore out feeding her. In my eyes she was like a real, live baby, precious to me, my very own child.

Momma told me she'd seen the doll in the window of Pizitz Department Store, and told Santa she knew a little girl who needed the doll. She'd even thought to ask him to turn the music box on as he was leaving because her baby liked to sleep late on Christmas and keep her siblings waiting.

In the toe of my stocking, I found an orange and some raisins still attached to a dried-up stem. Fresh oranges were a rarity at our house and I rationed mine, eating just one section a day and letting the juice slowly run down my throat. My miserly effort to make my orange last didn't pay off, however. There were too many sections and six of them grew green mold. Momma insisted I throw away what was left and I sobbed for hours.

As I grew older I realized our family was not a lot better off that year than we'd been the year of my birth. Daddy's construction job had shut down for the winter and he'd been laid off again, but somehow Momma managed the perfect gift for me.

I am still awed by my good fortune, the depths of my parents' love. I don't know what became of the doll, wore her out, most likely. The suitcase eventually fell apart, and Daddy removed the music box for me to keep and he later mounted it in the cigar box I kept my jewelry in.

# Chapter Four

More on Those Valley View Years<br>1939

After school, the children living in Valley View found numerous ways to have fun, although they owned few toys. After dark we played Hide-and-Seek. Afternoons, once our chores were done, we preferred Kick-the-Can. Or if we were lucky and someone had a ball with air left in it, we played dodge ball.

One summer night I was riding piggyback on Ann's shoulders, my hands lightly tangled in her long brown hair so I wouldn't slide off. She stumbled over something in the dark and we fell. As she skidded along the unpaved road my added weight shoved her forehead into the gravel, driving bits of rock and dirt into her scalp.

It took Momma hours to cut off her bangs at her scalp and dig out the debris imbedded in her forehead. The valley between her nose and cheeks disappeared, and swelling flattening the bridge of her nose, making her look like an Eskimo. She became furious with me for saying so. Although it really wasn't my fault, I felt guilty and later, was disappointed that she never offered me another ride.

One winter we had a really heavy snowfall. It stayed on the ground for twenty-one days. The streetcars quit running, but schools stayed open. Edgewood School's teachers who lived in Homewood had to walk to work and took a shortcut through Valley View to Edgewood, passing our house every day. Daddy saw them, and feeling sorry for their plight cut up old tires and turned them into overshoes for the teachers. The next morning, they gladly tied them over their own shoes and continued on their way.

When we tired of throwing snowballs, all the children living in Valley View decided to make a huge snowman. The ball for the base grew and grew, and was soon too big to set another ball up on, so we just kept rolling. It got so big the adults joined in and helped push the

23

giant snowball. It measured over eight feet tall by the time everybody tired and stopped pushing it around. Momma took a photograph with her little box camera. Long after the surrounding snow melted that big grey ball of ice and snow stood as a reminder in our front yard.

Another time, from the steps outside out kitchen door, the adults watched a bright light fall from the sky. I heard the story told so often I became convinced I had seen it, too, but Momma insisted that on the day it happened, I was too young to remember. I don't know if anyone ever learned what made the light, but some thought they'd seen a meteor or comet pass by right at dusk.

I loved washdays. Momma would build a fire under the big black iron pot and start hauling buckets of water from the well. She'd fill the pot over the fire, then fill two big wash tubs arranged on a wooden bench. Early on, she made her own lie soap. As times got better and she could afford it, she bought big bars of Octagon soap from the grocer. She'd boil the wash first, then rub strong soap on any dirty spots remaining before scrubbing each item on the washboard, sheets and white things first, Daddy's work clothes last, with my things stuck somewhere in between.

Clothespins fascinated me. Momma had two different kinds made of wood, and both made great toys. I liked to play with them. Monday was washday except when it rained. Then the dirty clothes piled up and on the next washday Momma would run out of clothespins and have to hang the sheets double on the line.

One day, standing at the washboard, Momma cried, "Ouch." She'd left a sewing needle pinned in the lapel of a house dress. The needle had broken off in the soft flesh beneath her right thumb. When she was unable to dig out the part broken off in her hand she went right back to scrubbing clothes.

By evening her hand had swelled so much Daddy had to peel the potatoes for supper. Next day, with red streaks going up her arm, she and I walked to the streetcar and rode it to Five Points to see the doctor.

He said there was nothing he could do, the needle would have to work its way through her skin. Soaking it in Epsom Salts speeded up the process, which took weeks, with Momma in pain and unable to use her hand.

Momma Rosie took over the wash, Daddy the cooking. Nothing tasted the same. I didn't like it that Momma couldn't brush my hair. She knew to be gentle and ease the bristles through my tangles. Juanita and Ann didn't mind if they pulled my hair.

After the needle worked its way through Momma's skin, Daddy made a quilt frame on pulleys Momma could let down from the living room ceiling on a rope, and on cold days the women gathered at our house to quilt. I enjoyed crawling under that lovingly pieced together canopy destined in the near future to keep some relative warm so they wouldn't get sick.

When Aunt Jeanette for married, Momma Gave the quilt to her. She was just a little older than Ann, and they were great friends.

Money was always tight, and doctor visits cost a lot, so we tried never to get sick. As the baby, I slept on a cot in my parents' room, but if someone ran a fever and needed nursing, the sick child shared my bed. I don't know how many cases of measles, mumps and whooping cough I shared my bed with, but I never caught any of those childhood diseases.

All was not fun and games. Every winter Ann got mastoiditis and had to have her ears lanced. Finally, the doctor said, "Your daughter's tonsils and adenoids have to come out."

"Might as well remove all my children's tonsils at once," Momma said, and scheduled the surgery for the end of that week.

We were admitted to Children's Hospital the night before. Barely four, I'd never spent a night away from home and cried myself to sleep. Ann climbed out of her bed to comfort me, came down with a fever, and next morning the hospital staff sent her home, advising Momma to reschedule her surgery in a few weeks.

Just as well. Three children with sore throats were probably enough. We whimpered. We cried. We begged for something to make the pain go way, but there were no popsicles at our house. The block of ice in the ice box couldn't keep the treats frozen, so Momma chipped thee ice and gave each of us a cupful to suck on.

My throat hurt for days. Then the scab started trying to come off when I swallowed. I stopped swallowing, afraid losing the scab would hurt even more.

Momma and I made another visit to the doctor that stands out in my mind. One morning she murmured something that sounded like she had a lump on her breast and wanted the doctor to have a look at it while I sat in his waiting room and behaved myself, so I got dressed and walked with her to the street car line.

At the doctor's office, ever so often his nurse came out to make certain I hadn't moved.

I finally decided the doctor needed new glasses, because it took him hours to look for that lump. It was about time for school to get out before the nurse led me to Momma's bedside. She acted woozy and looked pale. Talked funny, too. I sat beside her bed until she stopped throwing up and could stand without help. Then we caught the streetcar to Homewood and walked the mile-and-a-half home.

Momma was always stoic, able to withstand great pain. I inherited that trait, which has seen me through many bad times.

Sometime before I started to school I took sick with a bad cough. While I dressed Momma borrowed car fare from Momma Rosie. I don't remember the walk to the streetcar or the ride, I just recall how bad I felt and that my chest hurt when I breathed. The doctor said I had bronchitis, and should be admitted to the hospital right away.

That meant we had to get back on the streetcar and ride downtown for ten blocks, then walk several more to Hillman Hospital, where the poor people of Birmingham went.

Momma checked me in. My cough is what I remember most about that hospital stay. I felt so bad I didn't even care when they made Momma leave after bedding me down in a big ward filled with other sick kids.

The nurse said, "Call me when you need to go to the bathroom, and I'll bring this shinny bed pan for you to use, because the doctor doesn't want you getting out of bed."

While waiting for supper to come I befriended the boy in the next bed. After eating, I needed to go potty really bad and called for the nurse.

The nurse didn't come and didn't come, and when I couldn't hold it in any longer, I wet the bed. I remember clearly my determination not to wet the bed in front of my new friends, the shock of letting go, and the sudden surge of hot liquid soaking my bed. Once I started, I couldn't stop the urine flow. Or the telltale smell, followed by chilling cold.

I lay still, hoping no one would know.

The nurse finally banged through the door. "Why didn't you wait for me?" she yelled. "I'm the only floor nurse on duty tonight. Why couldn't you be patient? I don't have time to change another bed."

I didn't try to defend myself, but wished she'd shut up. I felt enough shame without listening to a lecture. I hadn't wanted to wet my pants with a boy in the next bed.

*Only babies wet their pants. I knew better, and this wouldn't have happened if she'd come like you promised,* I wanted to say, but held my tongue.

After the nurse spread clean sheets on the bed with jerky motions, still murmuring things under her breath I couldn't quite understand, she helped me put on a dry hospital gown, then lifted me back into the metal baby bed. "This is so you won't climb out," she said, and banged a roof made of iron bars down over my bed.

She left muttering something about "the little trouble maker" and slammed the door to our ward.

Cozy and comfortable, I went right to sleep. The following morning, that nurse was not around and the nurse who liked me and always came running when I called gave me a box of crayons and a coloring book she said I could take home.

# Chapter Five

1936-1938

The Daily Struggle Goes On

One day an encyclopedia salesman found his way to Valley View and left smiling with three promissory notes clutched in his hand. He'd convinced Momma, Aunt Edith and Aunt Jo to each buy a set of reference books on time. "You'll never regret widening your children's horizons with your set of Comptons' Encyclopedias," I heard him say.

A big truck delivered our books the next week. A bookcase came with them and Momma proudly arranged the red imitation-leather covered books on the new shelves. Even though times were tough, each week she'd squirrel away the twenty-five-cent payment due on those books.

When the Union went out on strike and there wasn't enough food on the table to fill our empty stomachs, Daddy would cuss the necessity to pay for those books and slam out of the house without eating a bite. But I could tell from Momma's pleased expression as she dusted each red-covered book that she thought the purchase worth the sacrifice.

On their anniversary Daddy surprised Momma with a battery powered radio and she placed it on top of the bookcase. For a while we used Daddy's car battery for power, which meant he had to hook it back up to the car before he left for work.

Shaped like a cathedral covered in smooth veneer the radio soon became the center of family activity on winter nights. Daddy liked to listen to the news, and if President Roosevelt came on with one of his Fireside Chats that promised an end to the Depression, we were instructed, "Don't talk, just listen."

I don't know how Daddy came up with the money, but within a year, the radio had a battery of its own. We had to regularly have it charged.

"Not everyone can afford the magic of radio," Momma told us, so most Sunday nights we invited the relatives to laugh with Amos and Andy, Fibber McGee, and Gracie Allen. And when my older siblings came home from church we'd all get a taste of the cake or pie one of my aunts had baked to show their thanks.

I was too young to understand everything that came from the radio, but I'd laugh every time Daddy or Momma did. I liked all the shows except "I Love A Mystery" and "The Thin Man". The music played on those shows frightened me.

One Sunday night in late October of 1938, Momma, Daddy and I took our places around the radio, ready to enjoy whatever it might say.

The program began with soft music and when the announcer started talking in a boring voice, I lowered my head onto Momma's lap. Then a frightened voice said, "We interrupt this program to bring you a newsflash from Grovers Mill, New Jersey."

I felt Momma stiffen. Where had her soft lap gone?

I tried to ask, "What's wrong?" but Daddy shushed me, sounding mad. He did that sometimes. I shushed.

Later, the same announcer said something about "forty bodies lying in a field," and Momma drew in a sharp breath. His tone scared me. I covered my ears. His next words sounded like he was being chased up a hill, which scared me even more. Reaching out, Momma took Daddy's hand. I buried my face between her breasts, but didn't make a sound. I didn't want to get sent off to bed all by myself.

A knock suddenly sounded at our front door. Daddy said one of those words under his breath that Momma forbid Little Robert to use and jumped up to answer the door. He came right back with Uncle Bernie and all the other Valley View men.

"Were you listening?" I heard one whisper, then Daddy asked, "Where do you think they'll attack next?"

He sounded frightened, too, and I burrowed against Momma's soft breast, my hands pressed tight over my ears. I no longer cared to hear their conversation or the radio. Even the music was scary, and the announcer's voice.

"Where are the older children? Don't you think they ought to hear this?" Uncle Ralph asked.

"At Training Union," Daddy said, sounding impatient, and I could tell that unlike me, he didn't want to miss a word the announcer said.

"If the world's coming to an end, I want my family close by," Uncle Bernie said.

"You think I should go get them, Sugar?" Daddy asked.

"Bernie's right," Momma said. "Whatever happens, I'll feel better if we are all together when it does."

Daddy pulled his cap down on his head. "I won't be long," he said, giving Momma a fierce hug.

I begged to go with him. I didn't mind missing the rest of the broadcast. The announcer terrified me and from the way Daddy looked, even he was scared.

We drove the three miles to Dawson Baptist Church in no time and Daddy climbed out of the car in a big rush. Some men gathered on the church steps beneath the light shed by a bare bulb stopped Daddy to talk to him.

"What brings you back so soon, Bob?" Daddy's bald friend asked.

"Some unknown force is attacking the east coast and I've come to take my children home."

"Oh, didn't you hear? That was all a hoax," the man said.

"Yeah, someone else was just here," another added. "Said what you heard was a re-enactment put on by some fella named Orson Wells. He called it 'The War of the Worlds'. You must have left home right before he explained. The program you were listening to was a special broadcast for Halloween. It just went off."

I could see that Daddy felt foolish, letting a silly radio program scare him, but since he was already at the church he collected my brother and sisters, and on the way home told them what we'd heard and why he'd come for them. They were upset they'd missed all the excitement. Little Robert especially. He thrived on talk of war and guns.

When we reached home, all the relatives had gathered, discussing how the broadcast had made them feel.

"Great sound effects. Tanks rumbling down the street."

"Yeah, and folks cut off in mid-scream. Even the announcer's voice cut off in the middle of describing an attack."

"I mean, it was like we were right there," Ralph said, slapping Daddy on the back. "I even looked out the door to see if the sky was red, so I'd know how soon those invaders would be here."

Not one of us thought Mr. Wells' Halloween prank was funny, and when we gathered for the family feast on Thanksgiving, my uncles were still talking about that broadcast.

When it came time for Christmas, both adults and kids looked forward to the holidays, the adults with dread if money was scarce, their siblings with the unfettered excitement of a child.

Decorating our house for Christmas never took long. Young pines trees and mistletoe grew wild near the abandoned mines on the hill above our house. Nobody cared if we helped ourselves or cut extra mistletoe for Little Robert to sell from the bushel basket Mr. Temmerson allowed him to plop down on the sidewalk and set up shop outside his drug store on December twenty-first. So as soon as school let out for Christmas Little Robert would shimmy up a likely tree, knife in hand, to cut mistletoe for all the families to hang and him to sell.

A few days later, without parents in tow, we'd all hike up the same hill, find a fledgling pine that met with Momma's approval, chop it down and drag it home. Daddy would build a wooden stand for it and set it up in the living room when he got home from work.

Then we'd string popcorn and slather gooey flour paste on narrow strips of red and green construction paper and make chains to drape over the boughs. While Daddy hung a no-longer-shinny, tinfoil star on the top of the tree, we'd straighten strands of lead-foil tinsel saved from prior years. The tallest and oldest got to hang tinsel. I just stood back and watched as the tips of the tree began to twinkle with icicles like the two-foot-long ones hanging from our outside eaves. The tree had no lights. Momma wouldn't allow us to light candles for fear of a fire. Her home had burned down when she was a child.

I didn't mind doing without lights. I liked the sweet pine fragrance of the branches. To me, each new tree was even better than the last.

Some years there was little hope of a Merry Christmas at our house until the box from the Georgia relatives arrived. One year the box held dolls with hand-painted China heads, arms, and legs, presents for Juanita and Ann. Impractical, in hard times, but guaranteed to thrill little girls.

Robert played with his gift, a toy gun, for a while, then took great pleasure in riding his tricycle over those China arms and legs. Goodbye fancy dolls. This happened before I was born, but my family repeated the story for years.

One year their package contained a sock doll for me, the homemade kind with two heads, one of them Black-faced and hidden beneath the full skirt of the white-faced doll on top. That doll took some getting used to.

One year Momma Rosie gave Daddy a subscription to the Saturday Evening Post, and kept renewing that magazine until the publisher couldn't keep up with changing times and stopped publishing it. We were not allowed to touch the newest issue until Daddy said we could. He had always read everything he could get his hands on, and now he had something of his own.

He really loved that magazine. Every morning he'd stick the latest issue in his hip pocket, walk out the outhouse. I think it was because it was the only place he could go and not be surrounded by females.

# Chapter Six

1938-1939

School

During the summer of 1938 Little Robert grew at least a foot, big enough to easily lug around the heavy bag of newspapers he delivered to homes in nearby Edgewood, no matter how cold or wet the weather. On Saturdays, he covered the route twice, the second time to collect from his customers.

In mid-July he came down with the mumps and spent several weeks in bed. Daddy delivered the papers for him.

When July 21 rolled around, Little Robert's birthday, I knew something big was up. Momma herded us into his darkened room wearing a big grin. Then Daddy wheeled in a shiny new bike. We all let out jealous shrieks. Little Robert's cheeks were so swollen he couldn't smile, it even hurt him to grin, but I'll never forget the way his eyes grew bright even though he couldn't get out of bed and test his new bike.

That day was special. My parents didn't usually make a big thing about birthdays. There were just too many of us, but the money Little Robert brought home helped Momma make ends meet. He would soon be giving me a ride to school on his bike, for Momma insisted I was too young to walk with my sisters, even though they had walked to school at my age.

A few days before school started, when Momma came home from shopping and we'd tried on my new dresses, the ones she'd had on layaway, she said, "Marion, it's your birthday. Today you're six years old and I bought you a present. Be careful and don't drop it. It'll break," she said, and placed a black and white ceramic puppy in my hands. He was sitting back on his haunches, grinning at me, his little red tongue drooping from his mouth. The narrow slit behind his ears for coins barely showed.

I had fun showing the bank to my uncles, who all shared their pennies with me. A rubber stopper under the puppy's belly allowed me to remove the coins, a game I constantly played to see if I'd counted my loot wrong. I'd also talk to my cheerful-looking puppy and pretend to feed him like a real dog.

If I promised to be careful with an encyclopedia while she was bent over the sewing machine, Momma would allow me to thumb through one of her books. That's how I came across lots of picture of dogs. I showed those images to my bank. I thought he especially liked the black and white dogs.

"These are pictures of every dog in the whole world," I told him, then saw Momma looking at me with a smile. "I'm widening his horizons," I told her, although I had no idea what whose words meant. "So someday I'm can own a zoo."

"I can't wait for you to start school," she said. "There's so much for you to learn."

Before I was really ready for it, that time came, and teary-eyed, Momma stood at my side as Miss Hodnett, my teacher, lined the first-graders up outside her room. She was so tall the bun on top of her head seemed to brush the ceiling, but she gave me a sweet smile, took my hand in hers, and welcomed me to her class. I gave Momma one final wave and followed my teacher inside, half-way wishing I could walk back home with Momma.

Although frightened at first by my teacher's height—no one in my family was that tall or that nice to me—I fell hopelessly in love with my teacher and with school.

Little Robert was in seventh grade that year and rode me to school on his bike. Each morning he'd lift me up on the handle bars, caution me to keep my feet away from the front wheel so my toes wouldn't get caught in the spokes, then take off pedaling his bike down our bumpy road.

We lived at least three miles from the school, he had to dodge the rocks in the rutted road that wound past Momma Rosie's house on the first leg of our trip. From there the downhill road twisted through the woods, then crossed the ditch where, if Robert forgot to go slow, mud splashed on my clean dress.

Once out of the woods, we came to the paved road and I knew to get ready to go down the big hill. Robert's speed on the hill sucked my breath away. I had to muster up my courage, pretend that flying down the steep hill with the wind whistling past my ears didn't frighten me, even though it did. Robert loved to hit the dip at the bottom of the hill at full speed. We never wrecked, but came close often enough to keep me convinced we would.

In the winter the downhill ride chilled me to the bone, and without me asking, my brother covered my bare hands with his. I can't remember if he wore gloves. Probably not, but he always remembered to keep my hands warm.

For the next few blocks, we rode past pretty houses, then came to the busy street near the school where patrol boys dressed in white and wearing red banners across their chests blew loud whistles to stop traffic and let us cross to the school. It made me feel important, all those cars halting for Robert to dismount and push his bike across the street with me on his handlebars.

He'd walk his bike to the primary play area where on lucky days I'd smoothly slide to the ground. On unlucky days my panties would catch on the nut holding the handlebars in place and I'd need Robert's help getting free or I'd rip my new panties.

Every morning he'd repeat the same speech: "Stay on the primary playground until I come for you after school."

Edgewood School had a rule against riding bikes on the school ground. If we were running late Robert didn't observe the rule and the crossing guards turned in his name for detention. When that happened, he would be late coming for me. I'd wait, and wait, and wait.

Before school, I played in the primary area until the bell rang, then lined up and marched in with my class. For the first few weeks it seemed like all I learned in school was how to line up, to go to the rest room, get a drink, and go to recess or lunch.

We made straight lines.

If I was lucky, on the way back from lunch I passed Little Robert in the hall on his way to lunch. I always waved and even though he kept his eyes straight ahead and pretended not to notice me, a small smile played around his mouth.

Miss Hodnett had taught all my siblings in first grade and I was lucky to get her for my teacher.

The school district published a list of school supplies in the newspaper, things the parents of all students were expected to provide for their children. A large jar of paste, Crayola crayons in the eight primary colors—no other brand was allowed, a package of construction paper, tablet, pencil and ruler were a few of those things. Siblings attending the same school could not share, so for weeks before school started Momma stretched the food money to cover the cost of all the supplies her four children needed the first day. Momma Rosie gave each of us a book satchel to carry our hoard in.

"More tablets and pencils can be purchased in the school supply room," Miss Hodnett explained the first day, "but we expect your paste and crayons to last all year."

If I was careless and didn't screw the lid on right, the paste would get hard, Momma warned. Sometimes the lid stuck and I couldn't get it off. Teacher helped.

When I finished a desk assignment early, I'd trace around the paste lid on tablet paper, making overlapping circles, then color them using every crayon in my box. Violet was my favorite color and I saved it for special things like flowers and dresses. I used up the blue and the red crayon first.

Other times I sat quietly in my seat waiting for reading class to begin. I liked learning a new word, writing it in my table with the big wide lines, then adding a flash card of the new word to my growing stack. We didn't divide up into groups. All students learned each new thing at the same time, and no one was left behind.

After reading, we lined up and walked to lunch. The noise and confusion in the halls frightened me, all those lines of students coming and going. I kept an eye on my teacher leading our line. Tall and skinny, she stood above the crowd and I didn't once get lost. To me she seemed older than Momma Rosie, whose children had children of their own while Miss Hodnett had none. She wore wire-rimmed glasses and her hair pulled back into a bun that made her look mean, but she was always sweet to me. After the first few days I wasn't afraid of her any more at all.

After memorizing all the letters and practicing making them, then learning phonics—the sound two letters shoved together make – suddenly I could read. Sometime after Christmas, those phonics became words I could sound out. The first time I read straight through the primer in my desk – a story about a boy, a girl, and a dog—a whole new world opened up to me.

Miss Hodnett let me take an outdated primer home and read to my family about Dick and Jane and the trouble their dog Spot got into. My family quickly tired of hearing about them from me.

One day I asked Miss Hodnett, whom I both loved and admired, "What turns you into a teacher?"

"A lot of schooling."

"Like I'm getting here?"

"I guess you could say that. I kept learning right through many years of school, and college, too."

Right then I decided to be a teacher just like her as soon as I found out where college was.

That February, a boy in my class invited everyone in both first grade classes to his after-school birthday party in the cafeteria.

"Your friends will bring this boy a present. We can't afford to buy him a present," Momma said after reading my invitation. "Your daddy is out of work and you can't go to this party without taking a present."

"I'll be the only one who doesn't go," I wailed.

Later she said, "There is one way you could go to the party. You could give him your doggie bank. If I carefully wash it, it will look new," and I realized Momma wanted me to go to the party as much as I wanted to go.

But did I want to go bad enough to give up my bank? Yes, even though it would break my heart.

The day before the party I sadly watched Momma remove the eighteen cents I'd saved in my bank and scrub my China puppy until it shined like new. Then he disappeared beneath crinkled wrapping paper held closed by my prettiest hair ribbon Momma had flattened the ribbon with the flatiron she heated on the wood stove.

I had never been to a birthday party. After Pin The Tail on the Donkey and cake and ice cream, his parents placed two ribbon-bedecked wash tubs on the table, one marked Girls, the other Boys, and instructed each of us to grab a ribbon and pull. I don't remember what prize I drew, I just remember thinking nothing could replace my bank.

Later, I watched sadly as my friend opened my present, knowing I'd never see my dog bank again.

"The best presents are those we give away," Momma had told me. I didn't for even a minute believe her. I had given away something precious, had surrendered my most prized possession. Nothing would ever take my puppy's place in my heart.

# Chapter Seven

Widening Horizons
1940-1941

I entered second grade in September, delighted that like my siblings, I was in Mrs. Ware's room. But after just two weeks the principal stopped at my desk and whispered, "Bring all your things."

I followed her across the hall to the room taught by a tight-lipped woman who looked mean every time I passed her in the hall. Mrs. Ware had a big, soft lap and she didn't mind if I crawled up in it. Not this teacher. Like the headless horseman Little Robert liked to read to us about, this teacher was made up of skin and bones. She had no lap at all and didn't even smile to welcome me to her classroom.

I didn't want her for my teacher and for days, when she wasn't looking, tears ran down my face.

After about a week of tears, the principal moved me back to Mrs. Ware's class. My friend Madge Ray moved across the hall instead of me, and those of us in Mrs. Ware's room started using flash cards to improve our arithmetic.

For Christmas Aunt Edith gave me a present I would never forget. All the girls in second grade wore rings but me. I hadn't told my aunt I longed for one, but somehow, she guessed. My ring had a beautiful blue stone set in gold and I proudly wore it every day. I took if off to wash dishes and polished it on my nightie every night.

At school, I couldn't stand to be dirty and each day at the end of recess, I'd ask permission to wash my hands. Nothing equaled the feel of nice clean water running over my hands. At home I had to wash my hands in a pan of water someone else had washed in, too.

One day, two third grade girls came into the restroom to change the water in a goldfish bowl. I watched them for a while, then took off the ring I'd only had a few weeks. The sparkling blue jewel winked up from my palm.

I had been careful not to get it dirty, so it didn't need washing. I laid it by the sink, then soaped and rinsed my hands, twice, while I admired the goldfish swimming around in their clean glass bowl, keeping an eye on my ring at the same time.

We didn't have powdered soap at our house, the kind that squirted right onto your hands and made bubbly lather on my hands. We used bars of Octagon, or the strong lye soap Momma made, so at school I took my time washing my hands, separating my palms, seeing how big a bubble I could blow.

Finally, with the water still running, but the soap all rinsed off, I reached for my ring. The bell rang for first lunch, startling me. My hand jerked.

I dropped the ring when I reached to turn off the water, but my wet hands slipped off the knob.

The stream of running water pushed my beautiful ring right down the sink drain. And the nicest present Aunt Edith had ever given me disappeared.

I cried so hard the teacher rang for the janitor. He told me he went to school just to learn how to find lost rings. He must not have paid close enough attention to his teacher, because he couldn't find my ring although I twice showed him which sink swallowed it.

Momma was as upset about the loss as I was and we cried together about the sink eating my ring for lunch.

I idolized my brother, who still rode me to school every day, and still waited each afternoon on the playground for him to come for me.

One afternoon he never came.

I liked to play in the loose gravel in the primary students' area and didn't begin to get scared until the rest of the playground grew quiet and I discovered I was all alone. I waited some more, and still he didn't come.

I walked over to the heavy double doors he usually came out if he got detention and tried to go inside. The door wouldn't open. It was locked.

Then a teacher saw me hanging around outside and called, "Go home, little girl. Everyone else has gone and your mother will worry about you."

I'd missed my sisters, who always walked home together, knowing Little Robert would give me a ride. I didn't know where he was, but that teacher insisted I get my things and go home.

Walk home alone? Momma wouldn't like it if I did, but what else could I do? I had a long way to walk and it would soon be dark.

My book satchel banged my leg as I hurried across the busy street running by Temmerson's Drug Store, turned two corners and crossed the streetcar trestle behind our church, terrified I'd fall through those wide spaces between boards. At last I came to the nice houses at the foot of the big hill, a hill so steep I couldn't see the crest.

I didn't think I'd ever make it. Up, up, up I trudged, my legs aching with each step.

Momma's friend Mrs. Thompson lived in the last house on the right before the pavement ended. Her house had a telephone and sometimes she'd deliver a message for us about some relative who'd died or needed us. On this day, she was pulling weeds from a flower bed and stopped work to talk to me. She even offered me a drink of water.

I told her why I was walking home alone, and she offered to drive me the rest of the way. When I realized I wouldn't have to walk through those scary woods all by myself I almost danced for joy.

Momma made a big thing of me walking home. "You're too young. *Never* ever walk all the way by yourself again."

Why was she so upset? Next year, Little Robert would start high school, would no longer be around to ride me on his bike. Then I would have to walk home with Ann and Juanita.

*What difference would one more year make?* My sisters and all my friends walked to school.

*Why couldn't I?* I wondered, feeling very grown up. It was high time Momma stopped treating me like a baby. I knew the way home.

Several years went by before I realized I would always be her baby in Momma's eyes.

When she stopped fussing over me, she started worrying about Little Robert.

Where could he be?

Daddy came home at his usual time and tried to calm her. "Sugar, you know how boys are. He's always home by dark," but the sun went down and he didn't come home.

"Let's eat," Daddy said and the rest of us did, but Momma was too upset to sit down, and Daddy never even picked up his fork.

After supper he went to each of the neighboring houses to ask if anybody had seen my brother. "None of the relatives have seen him since he rode by their house this morning on the way to school," Daddy said on his return, letting Momma lean into him while she cried.

I tried to not make any noise as I got ready for bed. Nobody slept good without Little Robert in his empty bed. I woke up sometime in the middle of the night because I heard voices in the next room and was sure Little Robert had come home, but in the morning learned he was still missing.

It was Saturday, so Daddy drove to Homewood to use the phone. He called Little Robert's teacher first, and after learning he was absent from school on Friday, called the Homewood police.

Two uniformed policemen came to our house in a funny looking car with a white sign on the side. They asked a lot of questions. The two of them even asked me some. I was a little afraid of them, but they were nice to me, and to Momma.

"You say he was wearing his Boy Scout Uniform?" one asked.

Momma nodded, close to tears.

"Now don't you be worrying," the other policeman said. "Boys his age run away every day. And if he's a Boy Scout, he can take care of himself."

We hoped so, but even though they said they'd be in touch, we didn't hear anything for three long days. Then word came that my brother had been found. In El Paso, Texas, and the authorities were bringing him home.

"How did he get so far away?" Momma asked.

"My guess is he hopped a freight. It would be just like him to do something stupid like that and not get caught." Daddy went on to blame himself, said he'd put ideas in the boy's head with all his talk about his hobo days riding the rails.

Next afternoon a car door slammed in our drive and we all rushed to the porch. Two policemen were helping Little Robert get out of their back seat. He looked tired, his Boy Scout uniform filthy, one of his knees bloody, but he seemed to stand taller as he gave us a shy grin.

Daddy questioned him. Momma upbraided him. Several times that night I heard Daddy say, "What?" and listened hard for Daddy's razor strop and the whipping I thought my brother deserved. It didn't happen. He got off Scott free after making me walk home all by myself.

After his homecoming, Little Robert looked different to me, more grown up in a way I didn't understand, and he acted as if he no longer had time for his little sister.

He'd left home because his girlfriend had invited him to her party, but he didn't have a Sunday suit or sport coat to wear. Little Robert took off, I later learned, rather than go in his school clothes, or tell his girlfriend the real reason he wouldn't be at her party.

# Chapter Eight

Vincent

1941-1942

By the time school got for the summer of 1941 our family's financial situation had greatly improved. Daddy had steady work, with paid overtime, so he promised to buy Momma a new car if she would learn to drive.

The two of them didn't let us in on the plan. Three times a week Momma would put on her Sunday best, send me to play with Diane, and walk out to the streetcar line, refusing to tell us where she was going all dressed up.

Then one day she came back all smiles, a new driver's license clutched in her hand. The next day she and Daddy went off to buy a car. She drove home a shiny, navy blue 1941 Dodge with Fluid Drive.

It looked like Daddy's job in Childersburg, Alabama would last a while. Right before school started, To put an end to his daily commute of over thirty miles each way, we moved to Vincent, Alabama.

Vincent was a small cotton-growing town across a wide river from Childersburg, where DuPont was putting up a gunpowder plant and Daddy was foreman over all the electrical work.

We were one of the last to move from Valley View, which was fast becoming a ghost town. Momma Rosie had found an apartment on the streetcar line and took a job sewing parachutes. Ralph found a job with the railroad and moved his family into a government-subsidized apartment complex.

I would soon be eight, and my memories of Vincent are quite clear. Hitler and his men were shooting at everything in sight in some place called Europe, increasing the need for gunpowder. That part was good, because it gave Daddy steady work, but a gunpowder plant is a dangerous place to work.

I was too young to be involved in the packing and unpacking, so I don't remember moving into the yellow rented house that sat on the busy highway leading out of the small town. Once we were settled, Daddy drove us out to the ferry landing to show off the muddy water he was ferried across twice a day to get to and from his work. We stood on the Vincent side while Daddy pointed out the various structures going up on the Childersburg side.

I had never seen such a fast-moving river, had only waded in shallow creeks prone to dry up when the weather got hot. Nor had I ever watched men wearing hard hats and carrying metal lunch boxes leave their parked cars and stand quietly on a rickety-looking ferry that expelled them, laughing and talking, on the other side. I never forgot the site.

I marveled at the wonder of light bulbs dangling from the ceiling, the sudden blinding light that bathed each room of our rented house at the pull of a string I couldn't reach. No more smelly kerosene lamps.

With only five rooms and the six of us, Little Robert announced he would sleep in the barn. Momma didn't much like the idea, and it took Daddy a lot of talking to convince Momma her firstborn would survive even though he didn't share their roof.

Later, when I read about puberty, I realized my brother, then in ninth grade, had needed the privacy a house full of females didn't offer.

Daddy had thought long and hard before renting the vacant bungalow set back from the highway and surrounded by cotton fields. A Negro family lived on the hill right above the house.

"So long as you don't socialize with the Randalls, the Klu Klux Klan will look the other way," our landlord promised. "Alabama's rigid segregation laws are not as strictly enforced in the country as they were where you came from."

I'm sure Daddy wanted to provide the very best possible home for his family, given the amount of money he'd have coming in each week, and our new home fitted his needs.

The weathered-grey plantation house where the Randalls lived needed a coat of paint, its first. Shutters hung at the windows in various stages of disrepair. I did not understand why I was not allowed to play with their children and constantly asked, "Why not?"

"The neighbors are Black."

"If you let me go play with them, I won't get close enough for it to rub off," I promised, to no avail.

A path started beside our driveway and continued straight up the steep hill to their house and the source of our water supply, the well in their front yard. How I longed to follow that path to the top of the hill and play dolls with those pigtailed, skinny little girls.

On wash day someone from our family had to climb the hill and pump water into the pipe leading down the hill to a storage tank. I'd beg to be the one to go up and pump the water, because I was curious about those children, but in the short time we lived there, I never grew big enough to work the pump.

My parents cautioned us not to talk to those children unless our pigs got loose and into their corn, which the sow Daddy bought from them constantly did. Daddy was working too much overtime to repair the fence and told Little Robert to fix it, but the task didn't involve girls, so he kept putting it off.

It finally got cold enough to butcher the hogs and put an end to them getting into the neighbor's corn.

I had no one to play with except my sisters, who only tolerated me, for they were almost five and six years older and thought themselves too old to be my keeper.

Little Robert slept in the shop someone had added along one side of the barn. He was happiest sharpening files into blades for hunting knives and molding handles for them from melted lead. He fitted the cooled lead around the unsharpened part of the file, then neatly wrapped strips of leather around the lead, making a rustic but comfortable handle for the knife, which he then wore in the scabbard he made and hung from his belt. I liked to sneak into his messy room and watch him work. He never once ran me off.

Daddy didn't like that Little Robert made knives, but most of his finished products didn't turn out very good. I never understood why Daddy made such a big deal about those knives, or why he and Little Robert argued about them so much. Their most heated arguments usually ended with Little Robert mouthing off and earning himself a meeting with Daddy's leather strop, a long strip of leather attached to a wooden handle and also used to sharpen Momma's kitchen knives.

The switches Momma wielded no longer impressed my brother, so when he was really bad she put off his punishment until Daddy came home. Back then, parents believed in corporal punishment for the good of the child and were allowed to do whatever they thought best without interference from anyone.

If one of us got into trouble, we girls all got a switching and Little Robert a taste of Daddy's strop. I suppose that was easier than trying to determine which one of us was at fault. We'd all claim innocence, but Ann liked to tattle, a despicable trait of hers the rest of us despised, and we'd all get punished. "For good measure," Momma said.

The worst punishment was being sent to cut your own green switch off the peach tree, Momma's preference for our punishment. If the switch selected was too thin, Momma would get mad and cut a fatter one.

*Ouch*. Taking our punishment was as much a part of our daily routine as getting out of bed, for in our large family someone was always doing something wrong on the faint hope he or she would get away with it.

Although we had electricity, Momma still cooked on the wood stove from Valley View. Daddy plowed and planted a garden, but we moved in too late for the seeds he sowed to mature before frost. Our neighbors on the hill had a fine garden, so we bought fresh vegetables from them.

Each morning Daddy walked out to the highway running in front of our house. He'd stand there holding his hard hat, lunch box and extra quart thermos of coffee, which he jokingly referred to as his staff of life, and wait for his car pool to take him away, and later bring him back.

He'd been promoted to foreman right before we moved, and he took great pride in his work. The men working under Daddy called him 'Fireball'. He had a reputation at work for hitting the ceiling if any of his men slipped up. When an electrician did something stupid and his work failed to pass inspection, Daddy would get hopping mad and his coworkers learned to steer clear until he cooled down. The worker responsible for his rage kept out of sight till then.

He got hopping mad at Little Robert and at us if we let the coffee pot boil dry.

Daddy got called on the carpet at work, too, most often for not wearing his safety hat. He despised the uncomfortable thing, but was expected to always set a good example for the men under him.

One time he came home with both hands bandaged and for several days couldn't work. While working up on a ladder, he'd grabbed a wire that wasn't supposed to be 'hot.' Five thousand volts of electricity surged through his body over and over. Thankfully he'd been able to kick the ladder out from under him and fall.

The weight of his dangling body jerked him free of the hot wire and he fell fourteen feet to the concrete floor, escaping sure death with only third degree burns. His voice shook when he talked about it. I'd never seen my father so shaken. I stayed right by his side for days, offering him water, and even tried to roll him a cigarette.

Our new home had several outbuildings besides the barn and I had fun exploring all of them. The ground floor of the barn was divided into stalls where the farm animals we'd sold before we moved would have had a nice, new home.

For a while, we didn't even have a dog. Then a Georgia relative died, Momma went to his funeral, and came home with Jim, a registered Fox

Terrier and beloved pet of the man who had died. Momma had fallen in love with the Jim and the widow seemed delighted to part with him.

Daddy said Jim had to stay outside, but promised Momma first thing in the morning he'd let the dog in.

As soon as Daddy opened the door for him, Jim made a bee line for Momma's bed. He jumped on it a few times, then repeated the stunt on every bed in the house. He didn't stop until everybody was awake, then he'd made the rounds again, creating quite a stir.

Momma wrote the grieving widow to thank her for the dog, and mentioned his actions that first morning. "I know," the widow wrote back. "We never could break him of that." It took some convincing, but Daddy finally got Jim to stop' by not letting him in until everyone was up.

The barn where Little Robert slept was located about two hundred feet from the house. Just inside, a ladder made of rough lumber I didn't like to climb on was nailed to the wall. It led to an open loft where my sisters sectioned off a playhouse for each of us, and divided Grandpa Page's child-sized furniture among the rooms.

Ann took good care of her things and always had the prettiest dolls and the nicest clothes for them, and even though she was not the oldest, if she couldn't have her way she refused to play. If she didn't play, Juanita and I were stuck playing with our own well-worn dolls, so we always gave in to her demands.

Even after Ann was appeased and the toys were divided up, things didn't always run smoothly. Ann would threaten to quit over the least little thing, so she always got her way.

One warm Sunday afternoon, we'd just arranged the furniture and I was sweeping out my house when the handle of the broom disturbed the huge wasp nest hanging from the rafter above my head. Those angry wasps came at me from every direction, stinging my scalp, my face, my arms.

I screamed and screamed, wanting somebody to make them stop.

My parents came running out of the house. Daddy beat Momma up the ladder, saw what was happening and told my sisters to take me to the house while he lit a rolled-up newspaper and burned the wasp nest. The flames killed the grubs in the nest, but further angered the wasps still in attack mode.

Daddy was badly stung and our quiet Sunday ended with him in bed, his eyes swollen shut, and me in pain. That's when I discovered Daddy and I are both allergic to bee and wasp stings.

Until the Fall of 1941, my parents had never taken time for outings, but in that fall they started borrowing Little Robert's and Juanita's bicycles on Sunday afternoons with me perched on the handle bars, they'd ride through the fields of dried-cotton surrounding our house. Even though Momma tried to shush me, I'd smile and greet every cotton picker dragging a heavy bag of cotton we happened upon.

In September, school finally started. All four of use attended the same school, a consolidated school for grades one through twelve occupying a huge complex. Compared to the school I had previously attended, this school looked like the college campus Miss Hodnett had described for me.

I felt small there.

Lost.

Then somehow Momma learned that the school needed a cafeteria manager, and she got the job. I suppose cooking for a family of six and a willingness to work hard satisfied any requirements they might have had.

After school let out each afternoon I'd hurry to the cafeteria where a never-ending array of sweets awaited me. While I waited for Momma to close up, I'd down a dish of ice cream and anything else I could get my hands on.

I was in the third grade when school started, weighed only thirty-five pounds and was thirty-eight inches tall. By May, thanks to those after school snacks, I weighed eighty-five pounds, was four-feet eleven and only grew one more inch in the following years.

Church was still very important to my family, Daddy was an ordained deacon of Dawson Baptist Church of Edgewood, so every Sunday morning Momma drove the six of us thirty miles back to Dawson and we'd make a day of it.

Momma always drove, even when Daddy went somewhere with us. She would offer him the keys, but he'd say, "Sugar, you drive." He told his friends he got a kick out of being chauffeured around by the best-looking woman in town, and I believed him. Momma enjoyed the role, even bought clothes to match her new car.

With nothing now standing in her way, she'd attend Sunday School and preaching with us, wearing her new wardrobe, then to lunch at Momma Rosie's, an aunt's or with friend's. After Training Union, followed by more singing and preaching, Momma drove home with my sleepy head in her lap, my feet in Daddy's lap.

Dawson's minister, Brother Edwards, eventually told my parents, "You should support the church where you live." After much discussion we moved our membership to Vincent Baptist Church and for the next few months that congregation benefitted from our tithes.

Two identical church buildings sat in the same block of Vincent, one street over from the main drag, one Baptist, the other Methodist. Neither congregation could support a fulltime minister, so every other week the Baptist minister preached. The weeks in between we'd attend Sunday School at the Baptist Church, then walk to the Methodist church to hear what their minister had to say. Baptists don't care much for proselytes, so it's a good thing he never tried to convert us the way Daddy feared.

All social life in Vincent revolved around the high school. I watched my first donkey basketball game in the school auditorium.

On Saturday nights in the Winter, we watched movies in the gym, while in the Summer the latest movies were projected on the corner grocery-store wall. You brought your own chairs and benches. The lucky owner of a pickup-truck backed it in and arranged the seats in the back to face the large screen. Those occupants were entertained by their close-up view of flying insects crashing into the movie screen before the picture began.

I don't remember anything about my third-grade teacher, but the morning of December 7, 1941, stands out in my mind, the Sunday morning the Japanese bombed Pearl Harbor. Ann, a seventh grader, sat by the radio crying as she wrote down the names of each ship those bombs sank. We huddled around the radio all day. The next day I heard President Roosevelt say on the radio, "Yesterday, December 7, 1941 – is a date that will live in infamy."

I had no idea what that meant, but I could tell it was nothing good. Using some of Ann's notes at school on Monday I reported on the bombing and the number of our ships that were sunk. I know now that she was concerned for Little Robert. and the brothers of her friends who were destined to go to war.

For Christmas that year, Santa brought me a shiny, blue Roadmaster bicycle, one far too beautiful and tall for my short legs. My bike spent all that Winter in the living room, waiting for my legs to grow longer and strong enough for me to learn to ride.

The news was bad as the war hopscotched across the Pacific. Wake Island fell.

Our school sponsored a War Bond drive, the President warned there would be shortages and encouraged us to save tin foil.

Daddy said, "It's a good thing we brought the new car when we did. I doubt Detroit will turn out anything for civilian use for the duration."

I had no idea what all that meant, but his solemn pronouncement frightened me.

The teachers organized a patriotic show. Every class took part. Thank goodness for that dress rehearsal. My skinny legs shook. But the night of the performance, when I donned my short red, white and blue costume I thought I'd found my calling. We marched once around the stage to the raucous strains of "The Stars and Stripes Forever" played by the school band, then marked time in place while each row of third graders filed off. Awed by the audience, I failed to leave the stage and my teacher had to drag me off.

Every Saturday morning Momma headed for Birmingham to buy supplies for the school cafeteria and any family needs, sometimes leaving us at home with a long enough list of chores to do to keep us out of trouble until she returned.

It seldom worked that way. As one, we'd rush through Momma's list just so we had time to get into that trouble and not disappoint her.

Ann and Juanita were fast approaching their teens and constantly worried about boys and about learning to walk gracefully for them wearing high heels.

On one of those Saturdays when our work was done, Momma's favorite possession, a ceramic cream pitcher in the shape of a cow perched on the living room mantle, solemnly watching us. Ann and Juanita were learning to jitterbug with a book on their heads. When I asked why, Ann said, "You're supposed to keep your upper body still when you do this dance and just move your feet."

After a while, when it looked like they were getting the hang of it, Juanita put on a faster song. I was enjoying watching their feet fly and them taking turns walking with the book on their heads when an argument broke out over who deserved the next turn with the book. Mere words couldn't settle the dispute. They scuffled. In the following melee, the book sailed right off Ann's head and sent Momma's favorite pitcher tothe floor.

It shattered.

Silence reigned as three guilty sisters stared at the bits and pieces of Momma's cow.

"She won't miss it," Juanita insisted and hurried after the broom she'd just put away. Like a seasoned criminal she swept the evidence into a paper bag and buried it near the trash pile.

Momma came home. In unison, we held our breath as she walked into the room. "Why isn't my cream pitcher Mabel gave me on the mantel where it belongs?" she asked first one and then the other. The lie we'd decided to tell didn't fool her. Only the truth would, and soon the details of the afternoon's regrettable events tumbled from someone's lips. Man, did I feel bad when Momma wailed, "Everything I love you kids somehow manage to break."

On Saturdays when we all went to Birmingham, shopping, Momma's dog Jim would chase the car for miles. She told us he'd soon tire and head back home.

No way. Not our Jim.

The first time, after a few miles of him trying to catch us, we talked Momma into stopping. Instead of turning back to take him home, she locked Jim in the trunk of the car.

He was really good. Didn't bark or anything. Momma got all her shopping done and we started home. That's when she discovered he'd chewed every wire in the trunk in two and she had no brake lights.

The next time he chased the car, Momma let him get in with us and drove him home where she locked him in the smokehouse. Secure in the belief the block of lead strung on a rope fastened to the door and to the wall would keep the door shut tight and prevent the naughty dog from getting out, she drove away.

When we returned just before dark, Jim met us in the drive.

Momma said, "Why, Jim Devil, how did you get loose?" She always called him Jim Devil when he did something bad. "And where did you get the big lump on your head?"

Little Robert checked out the smokehouse and discovered he'd chewed the rope holding the lead weight in two. "The weight had fallen on his head."

We never succeeded in breaking him of trying to follow the car when we all piled in.

I looked forward to those Saturday shopping trips. As the baby, Momma always bought me a surprise, whether I went with her or not.

Everywhere we looked in downtown Birmingham there were signs the war effort was heating up. Recruitment posters. War bond rallies. Parades. And gold stars began to show up in the front windows of homes, which always made me feel sad.

In those early months the war caused few changes in our lives, other than the government pushing for early completion of the plant where Daddy worked. That meant he'd soon be looking for work again, and us for another place to live.

My parents talked it over and decided to move back to Birmingham so Momma would have family she could call on for help if needed when Daddy's work took him out of town. They devoted several weekends to the search for a house to rent, dragging all of us with them.

After several meetings, Daddy finalized a deal with a distant cousins of Momma's, the Wright family. Daddy promised to make monthly payments on the three acres they lived on and for Momma to provide any needed care while they lived out the remainder of their lives in their old house.

This gave Daddy the go ahead to begin building anywhere he chose. Momma wanted a log house, so Daddy placed an order for logs with a company in another state. In the spring word came that because of the war all non-essential orders for logs were cancelled. There was that word again. I began to see what it meant, if not to understand what logs had to do with winning a war.

Now Daddy was committed to making monthly payments on three acres of land he couldn't build on and we still had no place to live.

The following weekend Daddy loaded us all into Momma's car to go look over Daddy's land" as Momma like to say, to his delight.

Unaware the trip concerned our future home, I considered our outing an adventure and those three acres a wilderness put there for me to explore. A small stream bisected the property at the lowest point. It drained the farthest pasture, ran right past the barn and out to the unpaved road frequented by dairy trucks. The minute I spotted that shallow water I took off my shoes and waded right in. Crawdads skittering along on the muddy bottom chased me right back out again.

Momma and Daddy were deep in conversation all afternoon. I kept out of their way, but watched as they moved in and out of the barn, talking in hushed tones. Daddy had his carpenter's ruler folded up in one hand and every so often he'd open it, measure something and take notes with the pencil he'd stuck behind his ear.

I can still picture him stepping through the barn door wearing a pleased grin, his everyday Panama straw hat—the previous year it had been his best hat—shoved back on his head.

"Sugar," he said to Momma, "I think it'll do. The tin roof is still in good shape. With a little hard work we can replace these barn doors with a good solid front door and lots of windows. I think I can turn this into a home we'll both be proud to show off." Then he walked down the far side of the barn, pointing out the place he'd cut a hole for a window above the kitchen sink.

The rest of what he said went right over my head. I was too excited to comprehend more than Daddy's hope to turn this honeysuckle-and-goldenrod wilderness into a place for us to live.

Momma walked him through the barn again. "The overhead beams are dry and sound."

Six-by-six beams supported the roof and Daddy stepped off how many smaller ones he'd need to support the floor and walls and scribbled the number on his notepad. "I'll put a bedroom window for us where the barn door is, and cut a hole in the middle for the front door—"

"—painted red," Momma added and they both laughed. Red had always played a big part in their lives.

I didn't doubt for a minute that Daddy could convert that old grey barn into a decent place for us to live. My father could do anything, like draw plans for our new home in his head.

He didn't need an architect to tell him where to put the room dividers.

"I already have the framework for a house within those sturdy barn walls," he liked to brag if a relative seemed unconvinced.

Dividing the available space into livable rooms took vision. That's where Momma came in. Daddy spoke in terms of two-by-fours and flooring, she spoke of a shiny white kitchen with red trim.

Every weekend for the next few weeks we made the trip to Oak Grove, hauling used lumber to our building site and camping out overnight. The rental houses in Valley View were scheduled for demolition and the lumber given away. Daddy carefully dismantled two of the structures so he could use only the best wood, then hauled it the five miles to his property.

We didn't have to be told, we knew his children would be expected to help Daddy on the house. My job was to pull out and straighten any nails remaining in the used siding. Sometimes they could be reused. New nails were hard to come by. Daddy and Little Robert climbed onto the corrugated roof and sealed the overlapping joints with bad-smelling tar.

Momma was delighted we were moving back. As a child she'd lived not far from Oak Grove and the family cemetery where they buried Papa Will was only a mile away from Daddy's property. She wanted the siding on her house painted white, the roof red, but decided the painting could wait. She'd much rather have a dry place to lay her head.

Unless it rained, we slept under the stars. At night Oak Grove smelled like all dairy farms smell under a hot noonday sun. The locals referred to the pungent odor as "Evening in Oak Grove," and as night fell and the humidity increased, the strong smell of manure became more intense.

Ann fought our move, horrified by the prospect of friends coming to visit her and being forced to breathe the fetid air. She readily talked Daddy into taking us to the movies or stopping for an ice cream cone after church on Sunday night, but she didn't get far with her objections to the location of our new home.

To her chagrin we made the move. Like our first move, I don't remember much about the move to Oak Grove, or whether any furnishings other than the long dining table and benches we ate on outdoors throughout the Summer made the move. Seems like I remember some household items like clothes stored in the barn to stay dry, that had to be relocated from time to time as work progressed.

It seldom rained at night, only in late afternoon. Late summer in the south it rains every day. We'd go inside till it passed. The galvanized tin roof didn't leak, but the harder it rained, the louder the metal roof talked to us.

Ann didn't like camping, and we camped out all that summer. Momma cooked on an open fire under the big tree behind the barn. At night we spread our blankets under the stars.

Saturday night baths created a problem that must have been overcome without a hitch, because we all put on our Sunday best for church and hurried home to pick up the building where we'd left off.

All six of us stood down front for the preacher to welcome us on our first Sunday at Dawson, when we moved our memberships back, and it was as if we'd never been away.

The next weekend Daddy laid second-hand joists to support the floor and nailed used tongue-and-grove hardwood to four-by-four he stood upright to form the outside walls. For a few days I had the entire space to perform in while he and Little Robert cut holes for the windows. On Friday night Daddy came home with his truck filled with store-bought window sashes to go in those holes.

Then came the new front door, and the barn slowly began to look like a house. We celebrated each time Daddy got paid and brought home more building supplies, like two-by-fours and sheets of plywood for the inner walls.

Before the nights got too cool that fall, we were able to move inside and spread our pallets on the floor. Daddy went to work on a military base in Milledgeville, Georgia and came back every Friday night so he could spend the weekends working on the house. He showed Momma how to sand the floors with a machine so noisy I was forced to leave whenever it was on.

The next weekend Daddy spread a layer of varnish over the newly-sanded floors, but the dampness of the Oak Grove evenings kept the varnish from drying right. We stayed off the floors until Friday, in hopes they would dry, but when Daddy came home he said we'd have to sand off the varnish and start all over again.

This time he bought varnish, instead of trying to use up the old stuff he had on hand, and we were soon able to climb up into the hay loft again to sleep. The five of us trying to sleep in the kitchen so we wouldn't spoil those sticky floors had been a tight squeeze.

With the floors finished and the dividing walls up and painted—Momma and my sisters saw to the painting—the furniture Momma had on layaway began to arrive, a Lawson sofa, a blue easy chair for Daddy with deep, soft cushions, a pair of mahogany end tables, and the newly-slip covered horsehair sofa and matching chair once belonging to Aunt Jo and Uncle William overflowed from the living room into the space set aside in the far end for Momma's formal dining room.

While she was trying to decide what to do about the problem, another truck pulled up. Two men stepped out and unloaded a beautiful new mahogany dining room suite complete with six chairs, a China cabinet and a buffet.

When Daddy came home the following weekend, he couldn't believe his eyes. The living room looked like an overcrowded furniture showroom. "Well, Sugar, looks like you went overboard," he said. "How much of this can you send back?"

"Not a thing," she said, taking offense, "but I've been doing some measuring and the dining room furniture will fit perfectly in our bedroom."

"Wha-a-t!" He might as well have said, "No way." I knew that's what he meant, but the next day I saw him and Momma busy with his fold-up ruler out behind our house, and knew Momma would get her way.

On Sunday Daddy told his cronies at church he, "hadn't even finished moving Annie Laura into her new house and already needed to add on."

He'd do anything to please Momma and soon added two rooms across the back, giving Momma and Daddy a room of their own again, and creating a small spare room for guests. This would free the original space they'd slept in fto become a separate dining room, and save steps for Momma when setting out a company meal, as that room was closer to the kitchen than the space they'd previously set aside.

The government was having some old military barracks on a base in Millington, Georgia dismantled and advertised wood free-for-the-taking. Daddy sorted through the pile after his shift, set aside enough to complete the addition, and left it to Momma to bring Little Robert and pull the trailer, and tow home the wood. They twice drove to the base and brought back full loads, the only mishap, a nail in a trailer tire.

The big tree that shaded the back of the house made constructing the new rooms more difficult and its close proximity severely limited the size of the new room, but Momma couldn't bear the thought of Daddy cutting down her favorite tree.

First, though, he had to chop away some of the huge roots to make room to lay the joists for the floor, even though he built the addition a step up from the rest of the house so the floor would clear most of them. Momma cried over every tree limb she was forced to give up, to make room for her new bedroom. The walls of the addition went up within inches of the tree's trunk

When the addition was finished, Momma could put her hand out the bedroom window and touch the tree's trunk.

In the attic space above the addition, Little Robert built his own room, nicer by far than the space where the rest of us slept. He had a window looking out on the back yard, real walls, and a lockable door to keep us out of his sanctum.

Each of us girls had a designated sleeping area under the slanting tin roof. Nothing divided the rooms or hid the metal roof. Ann and Juanita had matching twin beds bought while we lived in Vincent. Momma bought my bed on my birthday, a maple one with matching dresser and bench. Her purchase bent Ann's and Juanita's noses out of joint. Neither one had a dresser of their very own.

Daddy promised he'd raise the roof before we got much older, and add dormer windows in the attic, giving us room to stand up in our newly-walled in rooms.

It never happened. My sisters began moving out before he had the time and money to do the job right. Their flight toward independence had one good result. It forced Daddy to stop threatening to declare a Sadie Hawkins Day to marry off his girls.

He painted their new bedroom pale green. The green spread with embroidered flowers Grandma Page had made for Momma turned her maple spool bed bought for her the day after they married, into a field of wildflowers, the prettiest site I'd ever seen.

Some years after they moved in, Daddy came home with a hand painted doorknocker that no longer suited the remodeled home he was remodeling. He mounted the flower-filled basket to the outside of their bedroom door.

Now I know he hung the knocker to give them much needed privacy. Juanita always forgot until late on a Saturday night that she'd left the hair curlers she needed to curl her hair for Sunday on Momma's dresser and was always trying to slip into their room without being noticed to retrieve them.

Daddy always took his weekly bath on Saturday night and afterwards, he and Momma retired to their room and bolted the door.

The fancy new doorknocker made everyone think twice about disturbing them.

# Chapter Nine

Expanding My Mind at Hall Kent School
1942-1943

Right before school started for the Fall of 1942 I finally met the girl about my age who lived in the house across the road from ours. I'd seen Juanita Hulsey cross the school grounds with her brother numerous times as they made their way to the lone house perched on the hill beyond the school. A year older and a year ahead of me in school. Her dark good looks fitted her name.

My sister Juanita's ash blonde looks did not fit her name.

At Hall Kent School, the fourth and fifth graders shared their classroom with third graders, but they kept to the playground for primary students, so my new friend and I didn't associate with them. Juanita H. and I played together at recess and whenever I could sneak away from my after-school chores, which was nice.

I'd had no one to play with all summer since my sisters were helping build our house. Now in their teens, they no longer shared my interests. Boy talk and the making of new clothes seemed to be all they cared about.

The newest Juanita to occupy my free time was so skinny her boney knees knocked together when she walked. She'd been raised with boys, and although she looked frail, was tough.

We'd race each other to the swings on the school ground. After school she used our secret hoot-hoot-hoot bird call to signal me that she was ready to play. This hoot carried a greater distance than just calling someone's name. Then we'd race to do chin-ups on the playground equipment or climb our apple trees. I remember listening on weekends for the call made deep in her throat and amplified by her cupped hands. She seemed to be calling, "Who? Who? Who are you?"

Momma didn't like me to call her first. She insisted it would be rude to call Juanita if she was helping her mom, so I'd hurry through my chores then anxiously listen for my friend's call. I'd answer back, and go ask permission to play. If my simple chores were done, I was given permission to play as long as I stayed close enough to hear when my sisters called me home.

We never played inside either house, only outside, unless Juanita was having an asthma attack. One day, standing by the bed in her sick room after she'd missed a week of school, I witnessed a severe attack.

She started gasping for air, making terrible sounds. I pretended she didn't frighten me, but she did. Her father hurried in, broke a special cigarette, and lit it with a match. The fumes of some pungent incense filled the room. In a few minutes she could breathe without making noise, but I made up an excuse and left. I used to wish I had asthma, so my family would give me that much attention. I know better, now.

Her house was too small for company. And the smell of incense hung in the air, making it seem as if the house was sick. Counting the kitchen, there were four small rooms. Juanita and her older brother had their own rooms. Her parents slept in what should have been the living room.

She and I were best friends for years. Janet Johnson was my best friend at church, Juanita at home and in school. Juanita and I seldom played dolls. We enjoyed tomboy things like climbing trees and seeing how many chin-ups we could do on the school's bar.

I remember best the fun we had outdoors. Our dogs Jim and Suzie were forever producing puppies. Juanita couldn't have indoor pets, but the Hulseys kept chickens and she gathered the eggs. I was afraid of our chickens and always got pecked when I reached in to steal their eggs.

When her asthma wasn't bothering her, Juanita helped me round up our loose pigs. "Swine from hell," I called them.

As time drew near for school to start, I began to pay more attention to the oddly shaped, white clapboard school on the hill beside out house, and my friend explained a lot about the school to me.

The side toward us looked unfinished and I later learned the Board of Education expected to add on to the building when the community began to grow. Raleigh Kent, who owned the dairy, had donated the property for the school plopped down in the middle of his cow pastures, so his children could attend school nearby.

The side of the building facing away from our house had character. Tall windows with green trim looked out on a pin surrounded by electric fencing to keep the dairy's prize bull safely enclosed. Three large classrooms and an unused cafeteria opened onto a long, wide hall. My classroom had a stage at one end. Sliding partitions in the back of the room separated our classroom from the upper-grades, but I could hear every word their teacher, the school principal, said.

Outside my end of the building a flight of outside steps led up to a narrow porch and then, inside. On the primary end of the building the steps were not as high. Between those two porches, the restrooms jutted out of the hall like some architect's afterthought.

But such a nice afterthought. Indoor plumbing. What a treat, and something our new house didn't have until the following summer.

I could almost step out my back door and onto the school ground. If I ran late, which only happened when I had a new litter of puppies to check on, I could dash out the back door when I heard the line-up bell start ringing, and be lined up at the steps before it quit. The principal, Mrs. J, held the brass bell by its handle and vigorously flexed her wrist to make its loud ring heard on the playground. She was in charge, and could ring the bell as long as she liked.

She liked.

Once she had everyone's attention she made announcements. I can't remember what, just that she loved to hear herself talk. The primary students lined up at the far steps. Boys in one line, girls in another, we took turns marching in. Miss Copeland., my teacher, taught third, fourth and fifth-grade students, all in the same room.

When Mrs. J finally let us inside, I walked inside looking straight ahead. I didn't want to get into trouble and always sat in the very first seat of a fourth-grade row. The third graders sat in the two rows of smaller desks pushed together along the blackboards. The fifth-graders occupied similar rows beneath the high windows on my left.

While Miss drilled the fifth graders in spelling or math, I listened. That year, I mastered both fourth and fifth grade work and was bored by the time I reached fifth grade.

The boys in Mrs. J's sixth and seventh grade classes were all bigger than their teacher. That didn't keep her from paddling them when the need arose. Sometimes she'd come to our room and mete out punishment there, too.

Miss C assigned the girls who didn't ride the school bus the task of cleaning the erasers every day after school. While we beat them on the stair rail outside, the boys sent to bring in coal would tease us, calling us teacher's pets.

The older boys had to take out the ashes from each of three pot-bellied stoves used to heat the classrooms. They'd bring the buckets back in filled with coal. A local boy came to school early and started the fires each morning so those high-ceiling rooms held some semblance of warmth by the time the school bus driver dropped off his load of kids.

A metal pipe poked through the classroom ceiling to vent the smoke. Students gathered around the stove to warm their hands and toes. "Don't stand too close to the firebox," Miss C always warned, "you don't want to catch your clothes on fire," but on really cold days she'd arrange the chairs for our reading circle around the stove.

Dogs were not allowed on the school ground, one of Mrs. J's rules, but my dogs chose not to obey her. Each afternoon I'd find them patiently waiting for me by the school steps and they'd race me home.

Mrs. J only relaxed her rule concerning dogs on the school grounds when our pigs got out. About once a week she'd take me out of class to round up our pigs.

Feeding them the table scraps was one of my chores. I had to climb high up on their wooden fence and hold the pan out over the top rail before dumping the food into their trough.

"That big sow and her mate have wicked teeth that can take your arm off, so stay out of their way," Daddy had warned me, and I did. The old sow scared me, but not enough to keep me from climbing back up on their enclosure to watch them eat. Our hogs had no manners, pushing and shoving, even biting each other to gobble the scraps. The muddier they were, the happier, and their stench didn't seem to bother them.

Rounding up the hogs when they got loose became another of my chores. Once they found a place to squeeze under the lowest bars, they did it at least once a day.

We had two dogs by then. A boy at school who lived nearby had given me a female collie-shepherd mix I named Suzie. She and Jim loved to round up the pigs by raising a ruckus and snapping at their hooves.

Although nothing green grew on the school grounds, the pigs who broke free headed straight for the school. It took us a while, and we made a good deal of noise, but with the dogs' help, I'd get the pigs safely back in their pin and that evening, if Daddy was working in town, he'd close up the hole where they'd escaped.

Our house had my father's version of central heat. As central as Daddy could manage, I suppose. He installed the wood burning cook stove in the center of the open space outside their bedroom door.

To adjust the heat of any room, you simply opened or closed the nearest door or ceiling vent. We didn't heat the living room and dining room in winter, except for Christmas Day.

Heat rises, and once the family space was warm enough, we could open the downstairs vent and heat the attic where we slept. Daddy banked the fire when he went to bed, and with the metal roof, the attic quickly cooled off.

At bedtime my sisters and I clustered around the stove, soaking up warmth while we waited for the kettle to steam. With that boiling water we filled three fruit jars, wrapped them in towels and put one in each our beds to warm our feet.

Some nights my breath condensed on the underside of the tin roof and froze. It made pretty designs right above my head most mornings, but dripped icy water in my face when the sun warmed the roof.

Soon after we moved in Daddy joined the local Civitans, a civic club for men. Their members sold programs at the football games and Daddy began taking all of us, the reason the exciting sights and sounds of fall football became ensconced in my blood.

Momma Rosie bought Little Robert a trumpet so he could join the high school band. With the trumpet tucked under his arm, he'd get in the football games free. It took a while for Daddy to realize he was stashing his trumpet in the bushes and flirting with girls instead of sitting with the band. The two of them almost came to blows about it and Little Robert dropped out of the school band

As we went about our chores on Sunday mornings, everybody sang along with the Stanback Happy Hitters who instructed us to *'Turn Your Radio On'*. Weekdays, as Daddy checked on the pigs, he sang the spirituals Ernest Tubbs like to sing. I don't remember Momma singing, but from the time I could stand alone, she'd quote poems written by Edna St. Vincent Milay.

My sisters collected Bob Crosby's and Glenn Miller's latest 78 RPM records, then played them in the living room on Momma's console radio-phonograph while they practiced their boogie-woogie steps. War songs were the rage on the radio, tunes like *Johnnie Zero*, and *A Wing and a Prayer*.

I was musical, and every afternoon, out in our back acre, I'd sing the latest *Hit Parade* songs at the top of my voice. I can't remember how it started, but I was soon standing in front of my Sunday School class and my classmates at school, waving my arm to the music and leading them in song.

The first time the students put on *a Parents' Night program*, Mrs. J asked me to prepare a patriotic solo to sing. Don Goodwin, who always managed to sit next to me although he was a year ahead of me in school, volunteered his mother to play the piano while I sang. Several times a week we'd practiced my solo.

Those practices always went fine. The performance was a different story. When my parents walked over to the school that night, our dogs followed them. During the program, I'd just sung, *'The kids all called him Johnnie Zero,* when Jim Devil marched right down the center aisle, sat down at my feet and proceeded to howl in tune with my singing, the way he howled when a fire truck went by.

Together, we brought down the house.


With the United States involved in fighting across two oceans, Birmingham finally enjoyed a boom. As able-bodied men signed up to help Uncle Sam, young women and old men were stepping up to fill their shoes. Students collected tinfoil.

Everyone was busy doing their part.

Momma read about a school in Memphis training women to do men's jobs. Even though she didn't have a high school diploma, she wanted to do her part, but had no job skills. Vocational training sounded like the perfect solution.

"Hop to it," Daddy told her, so she applied, and surprised herself with the ease with which she passed the aptitude tests. Within days of the taking the exam she received her acceptance to attend the school.

Then Daddy shared the bad news. The six-week class would be held in Memphis, Tennessee. Apparently Daddy didn't see anything wrong with that. I did.

"My wife needs something productive to take her mind off the likelihood of her son going to war," I overheard him say to a friend at Church.

Taking care of me wasn't enough?

Who would run our house while Momma was away?

With three girls at home, Daddy didn't anticipate any problems. Momma did. Her oldest daughter, Juanita, was a dreamer, and couldn't be depended upon. Too flighty, so the responsibility fell on Ann, now in ninth grade. Although still bossy, she had excellent homemaking skills, so Momma put her in charge.

She lectured Ann at every turn, explaining how to do the laundry, plan and prepare meals, and make corn bread—a must for Sunday dinner—to be served with the store-bought chicken she'd be frying for us after Church.

Momma's way of cooking was a pinch of this and a handful of that, but at Ann's insistence, Momma wrote out her cornbread recipe.

"Obey Annie Laura," Momma told us, and to her she said said, "If somebody complains about your cooking, tell the fault-finder to go fry an egg."

None of us wanted to be singled out and I planned to bite my tongue.

The night before Momma was to catch the bus, I helped her pack. I thought my mother going off to learn war work was a lark, and had shared the news with all my friends. I couldn't understand why she was so emotional about her departure. I loved to go on trips.

Right before lunch the following day Momma knocked on my classroom door and asked to see me in the hall.

Miss C said, "Of course," and I hurried out to where Momma waited, exquisitely dressed.

Quietly sobbing, wearing the new suit she'd bought for travel, Momma hugged me and kissed my cheek, something she hadn't done since I started to school, then she walked away. When I stepped back inside and my classmates saw the perfect imprint of Momma's lips on my cheek, they snickered.

It hit me then. I wouldn't see my Momma again for weeks! She would no longer be out working in her flowerbeds when school let out and I wanted to keep the memory of her kiss forever. The tears I was trying to hold back escaped.

Miss C noticed me crying and drew attention away from me by telling the class about my mother's "big adventure."

She'd always been my favorite teacher, and as far as I was concerned her thoughtfulness had just earned a new star in her crown.

Momma wrote us often from Memphis. She described how she had learned to read blue prints and wiring diagrams and to use a soldering iron. By the end of those six-weeks she'd know how to construct the harnesses installed in the wings of airplanes that make the wing lights blink.

I don't remember much about those weeks of Ann's cooking, except that she bossed us around a lot while fixing meals. Oh, and that she made delicious deep-fried donuts until hot oil accidentally splashed up on her hand. She got third degree burns and never made donuts again.

Saturday laundry days were tough. Until she went away, Momma hadn't let anyone near the wringer washing machine she bought in Vincent. She was afraid one of us would strip the gears and she'd have to go back to using the scrub board. No more hand wringing of clothes, but the washing machine wringer terrified me.

Ann was unsympathetic. She assigned me the task of standing opposite her and opening up the folds of things she fed through the wringer. Sheets smashed flat, and Daddy's pants. I was terrified of the water standing on the laundry room floor, and of the wringer. What if it ate my fingers like it sometimes ate Ann's.

A time or two the wringer ate Ann's wooden spoon and jammed the wringer as she fed the clothes through. When that happened, she'd bang her fist on the wringer until it flew apart and the separated rollers released the spoon.

My job was to guide the just-wrung wash into the rinse tub, agitating the water to keep the opened-up wash from making a pile beneath the wringer, unless Ann caught her hand in the wringer as she fed the laundry through.

When she did, real quick like, my job was to unplug the washing machine, another task that frightened me, because of the water standing on the floor. Daddy was constantly cautioning us about the danger of wet feet and hands around electricity, but with the washer unplugged she and I could take our time beating on the wringer until it let go of her hand, so I'd grit my teeth, say a quick prayer, and dutifully pull the plug.

Soap scum collected in the first rinse as I guided the flattened wash into the second rinse and opened out the folds.

Ann washed the sheets first and we soaked them in a tub of bluing for the last rinse. The lighter clothes came next, and Daddy's work pants were always last. The thickness at the waist of those pants jammed the wringer every time.

From washing the clothesline, to removing blue jay droppings, to hanging the clean wash and checking later to see if it had dried enough to start ironing, everyone pitched in to help.

The clotheslines were three long wires strung from the big tree at the back of the house to a metal cross-arm fastened to the wooden post Daddy had sunk in the ground seventy-five feet away. Juanita's height earned her the job of hanging the clothes. She could count on a sharp dressing down from Ann if she let something clean and wet fall in the dirt. We wedged a notched wooden pole under each clothes-filled wire to keep the lines from sagging. As soon as anything dried, the ironing for Church began.

Ah, the convenience of electricity. No more heating a flatiron on the stove. Everyone did their own ironing, except for Daddy's clothes.

Ann ironed those, because he needed to look nice and she did the best job, Juanita ironed my school clothes and Daddy's work shirts, and Ann ironed the dresses I wore to Church. Instead of doing his own ironing, Little Robert paid Ann to press his shirts for Church and for dates.

Oh, I left out a step. Argo starch cooked on the stove. "Not too thick, or the clothes will be stiff, and don't let it burn while you're cooking it," Momma had cautioned. Everything but the sheets and towels got starched, even Daddy's work pants, which were dried on pants stretchers and didn't have to be ironed.

If it rained on Saturday we'd be out of clean clothes before the end of the following week.

One weekend Daddy went to visit Momma. On another, she came home to visit us wearing white wedge-heeled sandals I hadn't seen before. She and Daddy must have had a lot to say to each other, because for most of her stay they sat together in the adult swing hung from a tree, their heads close together. Momma had all kinds of new things to talk to him about. Things she'd learned in class—things I couldn't begin to understand. All those new things kept spilling out of her and she had little time for me.

Finally, the six weeks passed and Momma's time in Memphis came to an end. Daddy drove there to see her graduate, then brought her home. The place where she would work on airplanes was not ready for the work to begin, so she had a few weeks to be our Momma again.

About that time Mrs. J started giving the four upper grades lists of extra spelling words to memorize. The first week we studied car parts—carburetor, clutch and the like.

On Wednesday afternoon, just before time for school to let out she'd line us up along the chalkboard in Miss C's room for a spelling test. If you spelled your word right you were dismissed, early. Anyone who misspelled a word felt the sting of Mrs. Jones's paddle, an incentive to insure it didn't happen again. I loved spelling and never misspelled a word.

At recess, Mrs. J walked around on the playground swinging her paddle as if she just couldn't wait to catch someone doing something wrong, or for the older boys to think up something bad to do.

One warm spring day some of the girls in my class and I picked berries off the bushes that lined the baseball field and until the bell rang to go in, threw berries at the unsuspecting boys.

Instead of emptying her pockets of berries, the girl who sat behind me in class took a pocketful inside, and during class started throwing berries at me. At that close proximity they stung. I asked her politely to stop.

She refused.

Rather than tell the teacher and get my friend in trouble, I crawled under my desk to study my spelling list, well out of her reach. This caught Miss C's attention. She sent both of us to the Principal, me for the very first time.

I came away from that escapade with only a reprimand. In Mrs. Jones's opinion, my only mistake was in not telling my teacher what was going on.

Me? Tattle?

No way.

# Chapter Ten

Indoor Plumbing

1943

Our second Summer in Oak Grove, following detailed plans published in Popular Science or one of those magazines he read from cover to cover, Daddy dug a deep square hole outside the kitchen to make a septic tank. It took them most of that Summer to finish the digging, mix the concrete one wheelbarrow-full at a time and pour the heavy, lumpy mixture into the molds for thick walls and a floor.

While the concrete lid cured, Daddy scattered gravel in the bottom of shallow connecting ditches he'd dug for leaching fields throughout the yard. "To keep the septic tank from backing up," he said, and his ditches worked, unless it rained a lot.

When all was ready he hooked up the bathroom toilet. The shiny porcelain throne had sat for over a year, useless, in the tiny space he'd partitioned for the bathroom. Until then, I'd had the daily chore of emptying the slop jar in the outhouse located under the pecan tree next to the pig pen, not my favorite task.

Then the toilet finally flushed right, and I danced with joy.

I don't remember Little Robert taking driving lessons. It's like he was just born knowing how to drive and work on cars. I don't remember the day he got his license, an event Momma certainly wouldn't have let us celebrate. She insisted it would be a mistake to allow any of her children to drive.

I do remember my first ride in Little Robert's convertible, a Model A Ford with a rumble seat. He drove it to school that year.

The war in the Pacific was heating up, and when my brother failed the eleventh grade and was told to enroll in summer school, he lied about his age and enlisted in the Marines instead.

He didn't tell anyone until the day before he was to board the train to Paris Island, South Carolina, for basic training, so there wasn't much

Daddy could do. I overheard him say he hoped the Marine Corp would straighten out his son, and in some ways I suppose it did.

Little Robert's sudden departure about broke Momma's heart. Her war job still hadn't started and she badly needed something to take her mind off her first-born's preparations for war.

After boot camp he came home on leave dressed in his Marine greens and looking smug. The kids at school got to see him in his snappy uniform and on washday I got to hang his bilious-green, G.I. underwear on the clothesline.

Little Robert wasn't little any more. He stood a good five inches taller than Daddy and insisted we no longer call him Little Robert, but old habits died hard for me.

He looked so handsome and proud in his uniform with all those insignia. He even showed it off at Church, a place he'd refused to go for the last year. Of course, he expected to have a nice car to use for the duration of his leave, instead of his Model A Ford, but every time he drove her Dodge, Momma would find something else either broken, worn out, or used up on it.

After his leave he caught the train to Corpus Christy, Texas, this time courtesy of the Government, to train with the Second Marine Air Wing.

When he completed the training, he was granted a short leave before shipping overseas and we drove to New Orleans to spend a long weekend with him. He'd insisted we bring his current girlfriend, and Momma was fit to be tied. She'd expected to have her firstborn's undivided attention, which he was determined not to give.

We stayed in an interesting old hotel in the French Quarter with lots of wrought iron balconies and stairs. One afternoon we all took a harbor cruise. That's when we learned Momma didn't like boats. She clung to the rail but wouldn't allow me to go near it, convinced I would slip on the deck and slide right off the boat. I didn't ask, but I doubted she'd ever learned to swim. Growing up, she hadn't had much time for fun.

I saw baby turtles for sale in a souvenir shop and begged Daddy to buy one for me. He thought the ones with painted shells would die, but let me have a plain one. We also bought a bowl for him, and a small can of dead insects to feed him. I named him Stinky and carried him home in a shallow container of water. I liked the way he moved his prehistoric-looking legs that ended in tiny claws.

Back home, I let Stinky loose to crawl around on my palm. I had to go downstairs to wash his smelly bowl under running water, and let Stinky loose on my desk while I cleaned his bowl. Momma gave me a job to do while I was down there and I forgot about my turtle. When I remembered and hurried upstairs, I couldn't find Stinky anywhere.

We looked and looked. Every so often I'd search for him again. About a year later Stinky crawled out not far from where I'd left him, skinnier than before, but otherwise, okay.

With Robert heading overseas, we finally got a phone.

Poor Juanita. All the young men her age at church had gone to war, but she was convinced boys didn't ask her out because we didn't have a phone.

The good news was Little Robert could call us, and he did, from Camp Pendleton, the day his unit finally shipped out.

The bad news? We were on a party line. Our phone shared a party line with three other families and we had to listen to four different rings.

In the fall Hayes Aircraft located at the Birmingham Airport finally got its act together and hired Momma as one of the first harness makers for fighter planes and bombers returned stateside to their new facility for major wiring overhauls.

Momma stood on her feet the entire shift in the upper floor of a metal hanger, working the afternoon shift in a drafty hanger. She suffered through Summer heat and Winter cold, started work at three p.m. and clocked out at eleven.

I'd get myself off to school so she could sleep late in the morning. She'd sleepily speak to me through her closed bedroom door when I came home to heat and eat some Campbell's soup for my lunch. We'd talk about school and anything else she'd missed out on or needed to know about for a few minutes, then I'd eat and hurry back to school for recess.

On good days, she left for her shift before school let out. On bad days, her car was still in the drive when the closing bell rang and I'd dread going home. When Momma ran late she expected me to wash her back, fasten her bra, find her badge and pack her lunch, all at the same time.

Sometimes I'd find her still in bed, and have to wake her. Momma's nerves had worsened when Little Robert went overseas. Her doctor had prescribed Librium to calm her. She kept a large bottle by her bed, and one in her car. Sometimes she drank the pink liquid right from the bottle instead of carefully measuring the prescribed amount into a spoon.

Mornings, everyone quietly got ready for school and work without waking Momma, unless Juanita dawdled and missed the school bus, which happened far too often to please Momma, who'd have to crawl out of her warm bed, dress and drive Juanita those five miles to the high school in a cold car.

The airport was all the way across town. The shortest way home meant driving through a black neighborhood. Each night Daddy set his alarm to go off at 1:30 in the morning. If Momma safely made it home on time she'd reset the alarm to wake Daddy at his regular time.

If the 1:30 alarm went off, Daddy knew Momma had run into trouble before she got home, and he would get up and go looking for her car along her usual route. One night he found her with a flat tire.

On another occasion, she was half frozen in the parking lot at Hayes because she'd left her lights on and her battery was dead.

The one time Momma really needed him, Daddy never showed up to change her flat tire. A courteous Black man stopped, offered to change it for her, and did. When she pulled into her parking spot by the front porch she could hear Daddy's alarm going off and never let him forget the time he'd slept right through the noise.

All my life, Daddy had just six bottom teeth, right in front, and none on top. Then those teeth began to give him trouble. He had them pulled and to our surprise, had himself fitted with a set of false teeth he wore home.

I couldn't get used to his new look, he seemed to be always smiling. His jaws no longer caved in around his missing teeth and he looked just like the handsome young man in the picture frame Momma kept on her dresser, a portrait made on their wedding day.

When he went to bed that night, he slept with his new teeth in so he could surprise Momma when she got home.

When she quietly crept into their bedroom, he sat up and grinned widely to display his new dentures.

"They're wonderful, sweetheart," Momma said, "but while you were at it, why didn't you go ahead and get bottom teeth?"

"I did," he said, then realized his lower teeth were missing and launched a thorough search of the bed.

When he couldn't find his teeth tucked into the covers, he climbed out of bed.

"His bottom teeth fell out of his boxer shorts," Momma told us, finishing the now often-repeated tale that always makes us laugh.

*

That fall Daddy paid a hundred dollars to a farmer for two heifer calves and a young bull. He planned to raise the calves for their milk and fatten the bull to kill for beef.

They became my pets. Their soulful brown eyes fascinated me. I named the young bull Blue Boy and pretended he was my horse. He didn't mind being ridden, and I was at my happiest on his back.

One afternoon I found Blue Boy on his side, and when I couldn't make him stand up, ran inside for Daddy. He called the vet the dairy used, a deacon at our Church.

After a brief examination, the vet sadly shook his head. "He's suffered a cerebral hemorrhage. There's nothing I can do for him."

Boy, did I feel guilty. Had my eighty pounds on his back been too much for that sturdy little bull?

Not long after, Daddy traded the calves for a used electric cook stove, which suited Momma just fine. She hadn't wanted Daddy tied down by milking duties again, not with the dairy a few blocks away and three able daughters to send there to buy milk.

Momma loved the new stove, the ease of simply turning a knob and watching a burner heat up. We accidentally turned the wrong knob a few times, melting the aluminum pot in the deep well at the back of the stove. After replacing the pot for the second time Momma ordered us to always keep a quart of water in the pot.

Daddy ran a two-hundred-twenty-volt line to the stove's new location, which had required minor remodeling of the kitchen.

Earlier, he'd salvaged some kitchen cabinets with glass doors and painted them the same bright red as the ceramic roosters Momma had happily arranged on corner shelves above the sink. Lastly, Daddy used some stinky adhesive to glue new, dark-red, inlaid linoleum to the kitchen floor.

Not long after, Momma bought a new, front loading washing machine. I liked to sit at the kitchen table doing my homework and watch my clothes tumble past the Bendix's little round window as the wash cycled around. If anyone put too much soap in it, suds billowed out of the washer and onto the kitchen floor.

One night I started a load of clothes and resumed studying. Suddenly the washing machine started thumping so hard it made the kitchen floor shake. Then the washer walked across the floor, all the while making this strange banging noise. Terrified, I stood frozen in place and watched it dance.

Once the washer reached the end of its electric cord, it started dancing back and forth, banging first on the corner of Momma's new stove, then against the sink. The washer had taken on a life of its own and I had no idea how to stop it.

Mesmerized by the washer's hypnotic dance, I screamed and screamed.

Daddy, working out in the barn, heard me, and ran the more than seventy-five yards to the house. He took one look at me, then at the washer, and pulled the plug.

Silence. Glorious silence.

Then, "That's all you had to do to stop it," Daddy said. "Too many towels in one load. The washer was out of balance. That's all. Nothing to be frightened about."

For years he had great fun telling this story at my expense.

By winter he'd sold the old cook stove and installed a used coal-burning furnace in its place.

I was almost never sick, never missed a day of school, and when school shut down again that year because of snow, I ran out of anything good to read. I didn't enjoy Daddy's *Life Magazine* and his *Country Gentleman* didn't appeal to me. We all waited for his *Saturday Evening Post* to come, to see if Norman Rockwell would make the cover again.

The Rockwell painting of the young boy who failed to bow his head for the Thanksgiving blessing stands out in my memory, as does one with a boy at the dentist, and one with a little girl and her wagon at a parade. I didn't like the patriotic ones. I tried to forget the war, to forget that Little Robert might be where boys-not-yet-men were being shot at, and some of them were being killed.

No, no matter how long snow covered the ground I didn't try to read those war-filled pages. I waited impatiently for school to reopen. I wanted to ask Mrs. J where she went to college and how much it had cost. Without knowing the cost of a college education, I wouldn't know how much money to save.

When classes finally resumed we had a lot of learning to make up. So many things happened so fast another year went by before I got the chance to ask Mrs. J..

One weekend soon after school resumed my best friend Juanita Hulsey's father, a man much younger than my father, suddenly dropped dead. He hadn't even been sick.

All our neighbors knew we were members of Dawson Baptist Church. Some even criticized us for bypassing the churches in Oak Grove to attend a church three miles away. Mrs. Hulsey put aside those differences and asked my family to sing at her husband's funeral. We weren't sure why, except everyone in the community looked up to us, most likely because my parents didn't work for the dairy, which put us a class above them, I suppose.

Singing at the funeral was about the hardest thing we ever did. Like everyone else, my parents sang hymns in Church, but their voices were thready, at best. My sisters never sang in the school choir. I was the only one who'd done any solo work. Of the sixty students who attended Hall Kent, my teachers thought I had the sweetest voice.

That's not to say I was an exceptional singer, but I *could* carry a tune, and when Daddy couldn't think of any reason to refuse the request, we went to the funeral home early to practice our hymn with their organist.

Practicing was easy. We sounded pretty good. Only Daddy and I knew the man being buried, but when we faced the deceased man's family over his casket, while the organist played our sorrowful hymn, we couldn't help but remember other funerals, and all our throats clogged.

Momma's soft voice was the first to shake with emotion. Then I looked up and saw a kid in the front row I didn't even know wipe away a tear. My usually strong voice wavered all over the place and tears flooded my eyes.

We made it through the song, but were relieved when the organ stopped and we could sit down.

Mrs. Hulsey had to give up their rent-free house since her husband no longer worked at the dairy. Not long after the funeral, Juanita's family moved away. She arrived at school on the school bus right before the bell rang, and rode the bus home in the afternoon, so I only saw her at recess. Her father's death seemed to have built a wall between us.

The Carter family moved into the empty house across the street the following week. I already knew their youngest son, Richard, from my class at school.

About two weeks after they moved in, I was awakened early one morning by a strange noise. It sounded like someone hammering in the house across the road. My bedroom was in the front of the attic and my window looked out on the street. When I pulled back the shade to see what the racket was, I saw flames leaping into the sky from the Carter's house.

All the houses belonging to the dairy were constructed of wood and at least forty years old. In minutes the house and everything the Carters owned, which wasn't much, was gone. A fire truck arrived just after the roof caved in and the men on it sprayed the surrounding trees to keep them from catching on fire.

The Carters moved in with relatives living across town, leaving an empty seat in my classroom where Richard had once sat.

The house was never rebuilt. To this day the old foundation and collapsed chimney are grim reminders someone's home once occupied the lot. Each April blackberry bushes and goldenrod fight with sweet peas and daffodils for a toehold in the overgrown yard, and each May white blossoms on a climbing rose twine across the rusty iron fence surrounding the lot.

# Chapter Eleven

Shortages

1943-44

In early November of 1943 we wrapped Christmas gifts for Little Robert: a miniature chess game, playing cards and treats, and mailed the package to his FPO address.

Our own Christmas was bleak, not from any lack of money, but because my brother was not there to participate. We all missed him, even though he'd caused my parents heartache most of his young life. Not even the fake Christmas spirit Daddy insisted that we show for Momma's benefit took her mind off the absence of her first born for long.

While they were in New Orleans, Daddy and Little Robert had made up a list of the Pacific Islands where it seemed likely the Second Marine Air Wing would be sent. They matched each island with the name of a pie. Each of them kept a copy.

Three months later, letters started arriving from Little Robert that dwelled on what he'd eaten for dessert. Apple pie meant he was in the Marshall Islands, a tiny dot in the Pacific. Momma seemed relieved to know his whereabouts. I wasn't. It looked to me like he was a longways away. What if he couldn't find his way back home to us?

Momma had extrasensory perception with Little Robert. Her special hookup with him made the rest of us jealous. I wanted her to have ESP about me, not realizing she'd know right away when I was bad. She always knew when he was back on board a ship and his unit was on the move. She'd walked the floor. Wring her hands. Sometimes go for days without sleep.

Daddy tried to reassure her, but her anxiety attacks would always last until a thin airmail letter finally arrived from Little Robert. In it, he'd mention the latest variety of pie available in the mess hall and she could sleep again, safe in the knowledge her son had his feet back on solid ground, if you could consider a coral-based atoll in the middle of an ocean solid ground.

Another time she kept seeing her son dressed in government issued skivvies, lying on his stomach on a table surrounded by men in white, and the hand wringing and pacing started again. Not even Daddy's assurances, "He'll be all right, Sugar," eased her mind. She was convinced Robet had been injured in combat and no one would tell her.

Nothing as exciting, it turned out. He'd raised a boil on his butt that needed lancing and hadn't planned on telling Momma about his embarrassing surgery until she perfectly described the scene in a letter to him, and insisted on knowing what had happened to her son.

He never saw any combat. I don't know what Momma would have done if he had. His unit never moved in until the fighting had stopped. The closest to combat was his battle to keep his tent upright on Okinawa during a typhoon.

Sunday was Momma's day off. After church and the usual fried chicken dinner, she and Daddy would sit in the porch swing hung from a tree in the front yard and daydream about the house they planned to build when the Wrights who still lived on the hill above us finally died. Everyone knew my parents were salting away their money for the day they could tear the Wright's old house down and build a new one for us.

Their dreaming and planning was frequently interrupted by the arrival of uninvited company. One time Momma Rosie came to introduce her new husband, Mr. Herrick, to us. Her sudden marriage to a Spanish American War veteran who'd lost several fingers in the war surprised everyone.

Momma took an instant dislike to the stoic man. I decided she didn't want anyone trying to take Papa Will's place, not that Mr. Herrick could.

Momma Rosie called her new husband Mr. Herrick until the day he died, but he took good care of her, driving her around in his old Willis with its coat of newly-waxed navy paint, and bought her a nice little house in East Lake with room for chickens and a big garden.

Momma never liked for company to just drop in, but that's what folks did in the South. Before the dairy sold and the road was paved to make way for the new subdivision, if a car turned down the dirt road running in front of our house, chances were good we had company on the way. "Quick, help me straighten the house," Momma would order, and each of us girls would take off like dust bunnies in the wind to do some pre-assigned task. If the company caught Momma still wielding a broom, she wouldn't stop until she was through and the sweepings were swept into a pile. More than once, I cringed as she swept the floor beneath our visitor's feet.

When I wasn't in school I spent my free time up on the hill visiting Cousin Warren, his deaf brother, Cousin Earl, and their mother, Cousin Jane. Their house had never been painted inside or out. It stood high off the ground on the school side and had dark, intriguing places beneath it. When I was feeling brave, I liked to explore that space.

The Wrights didn't eat the same things we did, and I the food Cousin Warren cooked made my mouth water, but Momma cautioned me not to ever eat with them.

One night when Daddy was working in Memphis, Cousin Jane took sick and Momma rousted all of us to spend the night at their house. We crowded into their one empty bed. That's when I learned the true meaning of sleeping at the foot of the bed. To make room, in case Momma got to come to bed, my sisters put me in the middle at the foot of the bed.

I've never been so cold in my life. Nobody slept. My sister's icy feet were right in my face. The headboard of the guest bed was shoved up against an outside wall and the little heat from the fireplace failed to warm us. The threadbare quilts covering the lumpy mattress barely shielded us from the biting cold., and the wind whistling under the floorboards blew through the cracks and froze our toes.

Cousin Jane didn't die that night, and not for several more years, although her bad spells came closer together and lasted longer each time. A medication prescribed for an earlier ailment had permanently turned her skin blue, so even on the warmest day she looked cold.

We'd always had a big garden, so nothing about our gardening habits changed the because of the war effort. Ours was not planted as a Victory-garden. Our garden was planted to assure we'd have food even if Daddy got laid off.

Each spring he would send word to Black community that Daddy needed him to plow the garden, then come regularly to cut the weeds down in our front and back yard all summer.

George was so skinny he looked as if he might break if the wind blew. He'd arrive on a big white mule, dressed in unbelievably-threadbare clothes.

Momma fixed him a hot lunch and I'd carry it out to him on a tray. She insisted his plate, silver ware and the fruit jar that held his ice tea be washed separately from ours, then boiled. I thought she was afraid his black might rub off on us until I heard Momma whisper, "No telling what he's touched."

There was always something needing doing in the garden, planting and weeding to keep up with. Every night after dinner my entire family trooped out to the vegetable patch and grabbed hocs. Until I grew tall enough to manage a hoe my job was to pick off the bad bugs, but leave the lady bugs. They ate the bad bugs.

Every summer Daddy's mother came to stay with us for a month. She liked to have something to do with her hands, so Momma bought thread for a crocheted tablecloth. When finished, the points didn't hang from the four corners of the table, so she had to work on it some more.

During canning season, she'd sit and snap beans or peel fruit and vegetables for hours, then make her way back through the house to her room to rest. She was frail and made her way through to the guest room holding onto chair backs and walls. We worried she'd put her hand on the hot cook stove as she went by, but she never did.

When the apples started ripening, my job was to climb the apple trees and toss the biggest apples down to my sisters' waiting hands. We called them horse apples, unlike any apple sold in the store, tart and green, but those canned apple slices made delicious apple pies.

One summer, the new jar lids Momma bought didn't seal right and twelve quarts of green beans canned in her large pressure cooker spoiled. All that hard work, wasted. Momma wept as she emptied the smelly mess. Like so many other things, dependable canning lids had become a casualty of the war.

Good shoes were scarce, but not-very-good ones plentiful and didn't require ration stamps. My Sunday shoes wore out a few weeks before Easter the year I was in sixth grade, so Momma bought me a new pair and let me wear them to Church on a dewy night two weeks before Easter. The cardboard sole came unglued and was flapping by the time I got home.

The next Saturday we returned those shoes and bought a different style. First time I wore those they pulled apart where the strap met the sole and had to go back to the store. Their replacements lasted for six months.

There was a shortage of elastic, too. I wasn't clear on whether they'd simply ceased its manufacture or if elastic had come from overseas and could no longer be safely shipped to America, but clothing manufacturers stopped making panties with elastic. I had to switch to underwear with drawstrings. To this day, I despise drawstrings.

We did all right with the rationing of gas and tires, since Momma and Daddy both held jobs considered necessary to win the war, but we never had enough coffee and sugar stamps.

Daddy still insisted a fresh pot of coffee be nearly perked by the time he turned in the drive each evening, and with Momma working, we better have potatoes peeled and boiling or we'd hear about it from him. The dogs' barking would always let us know he was on the way up the road long before his Model A, a four-door sedan he'd bought second hand, came in sight.

At our house everybody used the old Singer treadle machine with its bullet-shaped shuttle until long after the war. Ann made the prettiest clothes, ones that looked really good on her.

I had a red velvet jumper I wore with a red crocheted hat a neighbor of Momma Rosie's made for me. For years I wore that outfit for Christmas, Church and funerals.

One of Momma's friends had a daughter named RoseEllen, and Momma bought her outgrown clothes for me, mostly made of velvet and fashioned in grown up styles. The baby blue one with princess lines had a neckline so low Momma filled it in with lace drawn up tight on a string. I no longer outgrew anything, so I wore those dresses for years.

When I was three, my favorite outfit had been a red polka-dotted sundress with straps that crisscrossed in back and matching panties attached to the waist. I don't think I ever learned to put that dress on by myself. Sometimes I'd get both legs in the same leg-hole and fall flat on my face.

Red is not my favorite color, but with my light blonde hair Momma washed every day, I attracted a lot of attention in my polka-dots.

Maroon is my best color. When nine, I felt all grown up in a three piece taffeta suit with pleated skirt, a hand-me-down from Georgia. Later, I felt stylish in a wool, fuchsia suit with covered buttons bought at Pizitz Department Store.

Juanita was the one who suffered. She chose loud floral prints for her clothes, not the best a choice for her since she'd inherited Grandma Page's washed-out skin tones.

Our social life still revolved around church. Everybody knew us and had been to our house for church parties. Not good. If I misbehaved in Sunday School, word quickly got back to Daddy.

In the sanctuary, I sat with the minister's daughter. One time she and I got the giggles and Reverend Edwards stopped his sermon to make us behave. Another time a bee flew in the window. How could he expect us to sit still for that?

Momma bought Daddy a three-piece Sunday suit and made him have a studio portrait made in it, wearing his felt Sunday hat. She'd acquired a closet full of dresses and suits, but for safety wore tailored men's slacks to work. Thanks to women freeing men to go to war by learning to do their jobs, women all across the country discovered the freedom of wearing slacks, and refused to give them up once the war ended.

On cold days I wore pants to school, either the leggings to my snow suit, or the jodhpurs I wore constantly, pretending I had a horse, but I felt very grown-up entering sixth grade and decided this year I'd no longer wear long pants for warmth under my skirts.

The first day, I took a front row seat in Mrs. J's class with a mixture of excitement and fear. I didn't want to feel the sting of her paddle, but I did want to learn the things I knew she would teach me. For the last two years I'd listened to her lectures through the flimsy folding doors separating my class from hers and couldn't wait to show her what I knew.

She liked me, I could tell. Any teacher would like a student who raised her hand to answer every question.

One day Mrs. J started her introduction to the geography lesson about Alaska by asking how many in the class had ever been there? Almost of its own volition, my hand shot in the air. Thankfully Mrs. J didn't comment. She must have known it was wishful thinking on my part and went right on with the lesson, ignoring my boldface lie.

I wanted so much to be different, to stand out in the crowd, something I found difficult in a family the size of mine. I kept hoping I'd stumble across a birth certificate showing my parents had adopted me. I longed for them to have chosen me over my siblings, maybe even for them to love me more.

It didn't happen, so for the next two years I tried to distinguish myself in other ways. Mrs. J gave extra credit for reports written on subjects we discussed in class. I used colored construction paper on mine, and pasted cut out letters on the cover of my reports. Paper fasteners held the booklets together. Inside, information I'd carefully copied by hand from Momma's encyclopedias described Admiral Byrd's trip to the South Pole and Lincoln's Civil War. I turned in a new report every day and Mrs. Jones dutifully hung each one on the folding doors.

Every time the students put on a program for the PTA meeting or school board, Mrs. J picked out a poem or essay for me to memorize. One year I recited *The Night Before Christmas* to a packed auditorium, another time, *The Raven*.

For those programs I wore one of the fancy dresses Momma bought from Mrs. Kent, party dresses her daughter had outgrown. She already had a fully-developed chest, and for years the blue velvet edged with lace and the burgundy decorated with soutache braid hung loose on me.

I had a real routine I used when I had something to memorize. I'd fill the bathtub with hot water, lean back in it and repeat each verse until I knew it by heart. I ignored the desperate knocks on the bathroom door, until Daddy knocked and ordered me out, which usually happened about the time the water got cold, so I didn't complain.

Elocution classes were the rage for young ladies back then, and my privileged cousin, Mildred Ann, shared with me the pieces she'd learned in class, but no longer performed. I recited those pieces for school programs. My rendition of the poem about a mom letting down her hair won best dramatic skit at Church Camp one year.

Every spring, like clockwork, our sow delivered a litter of cute little pigs I liked to hold. It was not until they got older that I was scared of them. Daddy sold most of the piglets, only keeping one or two for us to fatten, butcher and eat.

The first killing-freeze each Fall, he'd hire two local Black men skilled at butchering hogs to do the killing and stringing-up of our hogs the next bitter cold Saturday. They'd set up for the slaughtering under the pecan tree. One of the helpers would separate the chosen hog from the rest, then shoot it or hit it in the head with an axe. I didn't watch that part.

Then they'd drag the carcass over and string it up on a limb of the pecan tree that hung over a wash pot filled with water merrily steaming over a fire. Scraping the hair from the hog's hide required hot water and a well-sharpened knife.

I didn't like to see the intestines and hid while they gutted the hog, but when the men began slicing off hams and the parts to be turned into bacon, Daddy would call for us girls to help. We carried the chunks of meat to the long table where Momma got busy with salting the meat, so it wouldn't spoil.

My hands got cold and I stood close to the fire whenever I could to keep warm.

Right outside the kitchen door Daddy had first built a bridge across the ditch, and then a smoke house. My sisters arranged the salted meat on open wire shelves in the smoke house. I don't remember us ever using smoke to cure the meat, just salt and the cold.

One year the weather turned warm after that first freeze. The meat turned rancid. Momma scraped off the bad parts and cooked the rest despite the funny taste and smell. We couldn't afford to let it all go to waste.

After lunch on hog-killing day, Momma would cut up the big chunks of fat and drop them into a pot suspended over an open fire. Later, she'd strain the melted lard into the scrubbed clean metal buckets Daddy's sorghum syrup had come in.

Later still, came my favorite part. Momma would heat the oven and make cracklins by baking some of the skin. The rendering made the house smell like overcooked bacon and my eyes burn, but we all loved cracklin cornbread, a treat Momma always baked to go with our first backed ham.

Don Goodwin, now a seventh-grade student, claimed the desk next to my six-grade one. I didn't think much about it until the school Christmas party that year. I hadn't yet discovered boys, but Don had apparently noticed me the day I entered Hall Kent and had always managed to occupy the desk adjoining mine.

For Christmas, the entire school drew names and each student brought some practical gift for their recipient and placed it under the tree put up in the auditorium to mark the holidays.

That year, all the students who caught the school bus in Spalding where the Goodwins lived, knew Don was placing two gifts under the tree, one of them for me. I didn't notice their eyes on me when I opened a pretty blue package with silver letters that spelled my name.

The wrappings masked a large, blue-leather compact too big to fit into any purse I ever owned, but I fell in love with my useful surprise the moment I opened it. My feelings for Don were mixed. Unaware I was straddling the fence between woman and child, I didn't return Don's feelings and from then on felt ill-at-ease around him.

School let out for the holidays as scheduled. I couldn't wait for Christmas when I knew I'd be receiving another stack of the Bobbsey Twins books and would finally have something new to read.

I didn't want to give up my belief in Santa Claus, but the tragic death of my sixteen-year-old cousin in Georgia forced me to. He lived in Columbus, Georgia and was killed while standing in the back of a truck on December twenty-third. His head hit the underside of an overpass. He died instantly.

Daddy took the bad-news call and Momma drove us over there on Christmas Eve. James looked so perfect at the funeral home it was hard to believe he was dead. His funeral was scheduled for the twenty-sixth so we crowd-up with relatives until then. On Christmas morning, even though we were all grieving, my cousins discovered Santa had left gifts for them during the night.

Not any of the gifts were for me

Momma said Santa didn't know I was in Georgia and she bet he'd left my gifts at our house, where I'd hung my stocking.

It wasn't until we returned home and she sent me next door to check on Cousin Jane's family, that Santa left my filled stocking in the big blue easy chair, same as always, but Christmas was never the same for me after that.

My belief was shaken, but I kept right on pretending Santa came to our house. I got to go to bed early on Christmas Eve and didn't have to help get ready for the big production Christmas had become at our house.

I liked to lie in my bed and listen to all the commotion going on downstairs, the rattling of gift wrap, the opening cabinets, and the hushed whispers while stockings were being filled.

The food preparations for the Christmas feast started on Christmas Eve. Our house was the usual gathering place for the relatives' gift exchange because we had the most room for a crowd. If, in the middle of wrapping gifts Momma discovered she'd forgotten to buy some relative a gift, a noisy search would begin that didn't end until she'd turned up something suitable to wrap and the rattling of paper would begin again.

Then Momma's hay fever would set in. She was allergic to eggs, and handling a hen turkey affected her the same way that roasting a fat hen chicken did. She'd sneeze and wet her pants, sneeze and wet her pants, until my sisters had to take over in the kitchen for her.

Aunt Edith and Uncle Bernie were always the last to come on Christmas Day, and always arrived in boisterous Christmas spirits and with a funny smell on their breaths.

"They've been overindulging in eggnog," Momma Rosa would whisper, and I'd think, *What is so wrong about stopping off on the way here to visit friends?*

My cousin Diane shared my love of the Bobbsey Twins. Our want list always included a few titles and when we got together on Christmas Day we'd compare gifts.

The Christmas of sixth grade the younger brother of the cousin who died the prior year drove his car into a support column for the same overpass that had taken his brother's life. *Deliberately*, some men at the funeral whispered.

When we returned home I discovered Santa had brought me a chemistry set. I built a chemistry lab in the smoke house where I could mix stuff that smelled like rotten eggs to my heart's content. Gun powder and invisible ink were more of my concoctions.

Another favorite toy was the tabletop, electric stove Daddy brought home from work. It heated food just enough that I didn't get burned. One time, while Momma canned green beans in her pressure cooker, I canned them on my stove. Problem was, I didn't understand about sanitation or the necessity for jars to seal tight. A few days after I canned them, I discovered my beans had spoiled. What a stink!

That winter school shut down for a week due to heavy snow. I tied old wooden barrel-stays to my shoes and pretended I was skiing, just for something to do. I hated not being in school. Cut off from anything of interest to read, I couldn't wait for the snow to melt so I could return to class. I yearned for my horizons to be widened, for the snow to melt, school to reopen and my unquenchable thirst for knowledge to be slacked. I longed for a difficult word problem to solve, a multiplication table to recite, anything to stimulate my brain.

On those snow days, when I ran out of reading material, nothing helped. I didn't like Daddy's *Life* magazine or *The Saturday Evening Post*. They were filled with war news, not with things I wanted to read, like where Mrs. J attended college, and how I could find a way to go.

That summer Daddy also built a fourteen-by-thirty-foot screened in front porch all across the front of the house. Warm nights, we all worked on it. Daddy strung lights so he could see to drive nails late at night. I gathered and played with the scrap wood, until the mosquito bites I'd scratched became inflamed. Thinking Merthiolate would stop the itching, I painted the bites morning and night until I discovered I was allergic to the analgesic and every one of my bites turned into a boil.

The hard core of the biggest boil on my side grew so large it should have been lanced, but you still had to be on the verge of dying at our house to earn a doctor's visit. My huge boil didn't make the grade.

Momma Rosie said a poultice of bread soaked in Pet Milk would draw the boil to a head, so Momma tried that. It took a week for the angry lesion to heal, leaving a scar the size of a quarter.

The new porch became the place where we entertained hot weather company. Our house was seldom neat, so we never invited people over, even family, and never invited company in.

Momma's friends Grace and Elmer Hines made a habit of showing up without calling ahead of time. They'd drop by while out on a drive, catch us on the porch peeling apples or peaches for Momma to can the following day, and offer to help. They had no children and Momma felt sure they preferred the eternal commotion at our house to the ghostly silence of their near mansion.

Momma had moved the recently slip-covered, horsehair sofa to the porch and bought a nice new metal glider and matching chairs for extra seating. The new furniture hurt my bottom when I sat on it wearing shorts.

That porch got lots of use. Hot summer afternoons I read on that sofa, and slept on it on hot nights.

# Chapter Twelve

Altar Flowers

1944

I learned all kinds of interesting things at Momma's knee, especially my love of gardening. Following the first church Training Union party held at our house, word got out that Momma had turned our yard into a floral showplace and she was invited to join the altar committee.

The five women on the committee met officially once a year to plan and order commercial arrangements for those Winter weeks when there were no blooms in the committee member's yards. The rest of the year they met unofficially every Saturday morning by phone and compiled an oral inventory of what each member was willing to share.

"My peonies are in bloom," one would offer.

"My roses are outdoing themselves this year."

Or, "If it doesn't freeze tonight I'll have some tulips. Didn't you say you have some, too?"

Each took a turn assembling the arrangement, but everyone shared what they had growing in their yard. Magnolia leaves. Privet. Dried grass. To us it seemed like Momma's turn came every week, which frequently made the rest of us late for church.

A lot of elderly and needy lived near our church and the church budget could stretch to cover more of those needs when the church treasurer only had to budget money for altar flowers in the dead of winter.

Even commercial arrangements earned criticism from the altar committee if what the florist provided looked skimpy or shopworn.

"Did you see those flowers," one of the ladies would ask over the phone.

"Never, in my wildest dreams, would I have..."

"Did you see that ribbon? It looked like it had been left out in the rain."

"I don't think it had ever seen an iron."

"Wilted when he delivered it, is my guess. If I was that florist, I'd have been ashamed to sit it down."

"A waste of good money."

"What was he thinking? Our members expect to see well-balanced altar flowers that are pleasing to the eye."

In late February, as soon as spring flowering bulbs began to poke their colorful heads up through the frozen ground, the phone calls from the committee would start in earnest again. If one lady expected to have King Alfred daffodils in bloom, the others searched for something white to fill in with. "It's not right to completely strip any yard of blooms," most agreed.

And come midweek, when the mailman delivered the Church Bulletin to every member's home, the bulletin always contained a paragraph that praised the altar committee. The ladies basked in the simple thanks. If a member of the committee didn't do her share of the work, the others took that member to task behind the guilty party's back.

Arranging the altar flowers meant Momma had to get up by six on Sunday morning. The few times the flowers were arranged and placed on the altar on Saturday night had not worked well. By Sunday some blossoms had wilted or even died. No. The arranging had to be done early Sunday to assure the bouquet would still look fresh on Sunday night.

If a member of the committee chose the wrong greenery, something that wilted and drooped, the arrangement was replaced on Sunday afternoon. To the committee members' horror one Sunday morning, the bouquet died on the altar with all the worshipers looking on.

The altar committee added those flowers to the list of blooms that did not hold up well.

When flowers were plentiful, two matching baskets had to be arranged, meaning twice the work. No easy task, making two identical arrangements, I quickly learned.

While Momma arranged the flowers, my job was to cut whatever blooms she needed next, strip their stems of leaves and stick the blooms in the bucket at Momma's feet.

When she deemed the arrangement ready, we'd load it in the car. Getting the container safely to the Church without mishap, especially in a two-door car, became a family affair. I rode along in the back seat to keep the arrangement upright. Two arrangements made my job more difficult. Always running late, Momma drove like a bat out of Hades in the unlikely hope she'd beat the deacons to the sanctuary and sometime the arrangement would fall over, no matter how hard I tried to prevent it.

Momma would drive right up to the sanctuary door, then send me in to dust the altar and make sure the coast was clear. She didn't like for the preacher to catch her still wearing her yard shoes. When it was safe, she'd bring in the bouquet, set it down, pick up any fallen leaves or petals, and scurry out again.

Daddy would be dressed and jiggling his keys when we got back home, a sure sign he'd likely arrive late for the Sunday School class he taught. I'd jump into my own clothes as quickly as possible and off I'd go with him.

During the years she served on the altar committee Momma never made it to morning worship. Her committee duties kept her away, but on Sunday night she sat with Daddy in their pew, admiring the altar with a proud smile.

Growing enough flowers to provide for the altar took all Momma's time. In the spring she scattered seeds of marigolds, zinnias and salvia. Petunias looked lovely in the yard, but wilted when cut. The perennial flowers had to be weeded, separated and given room to spread. Once a year she pruned the hedge, flowering peach, butterfly bush and quince to keep them from growing so tall we couldn't reach the limbs in bloom.

First thing every spring Nigger George would knock down the tall weeds and grass in the front yard with his scythe, but Momma didn't allow him anywhere near her flower beds. He was too careless. One swing of his scythe and the beautiful pink stalks of phlox lost their heads. Sometimes we girls were commandeered to help weed. Juanita always managed to carelessly step on Momma's new plants. More of a homemaker, Ann grumbled if she had to do yard work. Gardening was not something she enjoyed.

I did. One afternoon I was helping Momma transplant salvia and she caught my dog Suzie coming along right behind us, biting the tops off the new plants. Suzie was in the dog house with Momma for most of the following week.

In the Spring, folks driving by would stop their cars in the road to admire the colorful array in our yard. Our house sat way back from the street, with flowerbeds skirting the perimeter of the yard, and blooming shrubs lining the drive. A wisteria vine climbed the old rock-covered well Momma had paid seven men to relocate to our yard. In early spring its purple clusters completely hid the metal arch where the bucket to bring water to the surface had once hung. Drivers leaned out their windows to sniff the sweetly scented air.

Momma's camellias were showy, too, their dark, shiny green leaves massed with perfectly shaped blooms that had no fragrance and would not last if picked. Sometimes she wowed bridal shower attendees by filling a punch bowl with water and floating camellias in it.

The street in front of our house was eventually paved and named Cobb Street, part of the new subdivision being built on the surrounding dairy property. Out by the street every Mother's Day, long canes of Paul's Scarlet Climbers weighted down with fragrant red blooms trailed over trellises, clung to the bent-pipe arbor Daddy had made for them, and waved at the cars.

Pink and blue hydrangea and snowy-white snowball grew along the shallow creek that meandered through the flowerbeds. Violets and verbena clustered at their our. All Momma's bushes and the blooms from her dogwood, apple and tulip trees eventually found their way to the altar.

Glorious in their solitude, peonies looked best by themselves, their pink and white bundles of fluffy petals peering over their gracefully tapered leaves. Dahlias never objected to being placed in a mixed summer bouquet. If planted at different times in the spring, gladiolas would bloom all summer, their long spikes perfect for the altar when backed by magnolia leaves. Tiger lilies, Easter lilies and stalks of amaryllis each took a turn on the altar, some in riotous contrast to the serenity of the quiet sanctuary.

I never saw a gardening book at our house. Nor did Momma ever buy plants. At her Garden Club meetings members willingly shared their perennials with her and their knowledge of plants. She gained her knowledge in this way and shared what she'd learned. Each year, her plants multiplied, and the work necessary to keep up her garden increased.

So did the congregation, and in a few years the deacons voted to build a beautiful new sanctuary.

After the dedication of the spacious building, like the Methodist Church up the street, the sanctuary committee contracted with a local florist to provide the weekly altar arrangements.

The ladies on the altar committee just shook their heads.

# Chapter Thirteen

Post War Times

1945

In April of 1945 President Franklin D. Roosevelt suddenly died. Our Birmingham Post-Herald delivery boy knocked on our door with the Extra Edition of the newspaper put out to announce his death. Headlines eight inches tall surrounded by a black border reported the sad news. He was the only President I'd ever known, and I felt like I'd lost my best friend. What would become of our country without President Roosevelt at its helm?

It didn't take long to find out. President Truman ordered planes to drop two atomic bombs on Japan and, despite the horrifying newsreels of the destruction there was joyous talk of our troops soon coming home.

In August I spent a week with my cousin Diane at her home in the small town of Gadsden, Alabama. One humid night we came out of a movie to find the sidewalks crowded with people and strips of toilet paper dangling from overhead wires.

What's going on?" Aunt Edith asked a woman passing by.

"The Japanese have surrendered. The Emperor accepted defeat."

My heart raced. Little Robert would soon be coming home.

He spent a few weeks in Kyoto, Japan, more time than we wanted, awaiting the Second Marine Air Wing's turn to board a military transport.

Then he called us from San Diego. "I just received my discharge papers, and am catching the next train home."

He brought presents, pink silk pillow covers embroidered with cherry blossoms, hand painted fans with some strange-looking Japanese characters printed along the edge, a little wooden puzzle box that I managed to opn on the first try, war souvenirs for himself, a knife, a

105

sword, and an empty shell casing, and for each of us girls, sea shell necklaces.

He'd smoke and talk and smoke and talk until everyone in the family began to wish he'd forget how. He'd always argued black was white, but now he seemed convinced he knew everything, had seen far more than anyone else had.

His arguments with Daddy became more heated, over why he'd stayed out all hours in Daddy's car and hadn't bothered to fill it up. And over what he planned to do with his life.

The only thing they seemed to agree on was that Little Robert would help Daddy build a shop under the pecan tree, a building they constructed of metal panels. It was to include a room for Little Robert and an open garage where he could work on cars. Now that he was a veteran, he no longer wished to be housed with the girls

The barn, as they called it, went up fast in the shadow of the pecan tree and not far from the no-longer occupied pig pin. The building had a concrete block foundation and a slanted, metal roof. Robert's room sat two steps off the ground. Anytime he left his room he locked the door. Daddy built a workbench down one side of the shop and claimed half of it for his plants, the first of many tomato plants he started from seed, Tom's Big Boys.

All winter he'd pour over seed catalogs and each spring he'd try something new. Foot long pole beans, and later, earthworms. The literature promised he'd make a mint on them. Within a week Daddy's worms had disappeared from their enclosure, so he never knew if they died, the birds simply ate them, or the worms had simply moved on.

That Fall, Daddy installed a new oil-burning furnace in the open space outside their bedroom. This furnace provided instant heat, and best of all, had a thermostat and the heater could be left on low all night. No one objected to the funny smell, or to clean burning oil replacing the messy buckets of coal and ash.

Ann and Juanita were taking secretarial courses in school that year, since an office seemed the most likely place for them to find work. Daddy bought a portable typewriter so they could work on their typing speed, unaware that typing on a portable typewriter slowed a typist down.

I taught myself to type and began typing my extra-credit reports for Mrs. Jones. Their typewriter promptly became my prized possession, but if a sister asked nicely, I'd let her borrow it. Ann was taking shorthand, and wrote notes to her girlfriend in symbols I couldn't translate.

Every Saturday when Momma went shopping, she still left a list of chores for each of us. Ann would pass her tasks off to Juanita, and Juanita dumped hers on me. One day I got tired of it and chased my sisters through the house with a butcher knife. If I was punished for doing it, the punishment doesn't stand out in my mind. The event does. In those days I got away with far too much.

That summer my birthday fell during my stay with Jeanette and Ralph. My aunt baked a birthday cake for me, something Momma had never done, probably because there were four of us, and she'd have been baking birthday cakes all the time. Besides, Momma was allergic to eggs and since she couldn't eat cake birthdays weren't celebrated at our house, but everybody liked to go to the movies. Ann was Daddy's favorite, so we'd put her up to begging him to take us to the movies on Friday or Sunday night. Baptists believe movies are the Devil's work, to be religiously avoided, and Sunday movies were strictly taboo.

"Why can't we go?" she'd argue when a good movie we hadn't seen was playing on Sunday night. "We've already gone to Church twice today and are still dressed in our best clothes. Please." Daddy got a kick out of movies, especially westerns starring John Wayne, and seldom denied Ann's request.

Back then only one movie at a time showed in the downtown theatres, along with a cartoon and assorted newsreels. The best first run movies opened at the Alabama Theater, where at intermission an organ rose up out of the floor and a man dressed in a tux caressed a thousand keys. It was my favorite time of the show. Lyrics to the songs he played magically appeared on the screen and if you followed the bouncing ball as you sang, you wouldn't miss a word.

No matter what the event, Momma always dressed for a movie in her Sunday best and donned her newest hat, taking so much time to get ready she always made us late. She liked to sit in the front of the balcony, but if we arrived late had to wait with a throng of other movie goes for the theatre to empty and the next showing to begin.

About two months after the war ended Hayes Aircraft laid Momma off. There was no longer a need to repair old fighter planes, and we all felt sorry for her.

Without her duties as a supervisor, she seemed at a loss to know what to do with her time, except shop for new clothes for herself, but her purchases just hung in the closet, most with the sales tags still attached.

She began sleeping late and was sometimes still in bed when I got home from school. On good days I'd find her out weeding and I'd drop down beside her and help.

If she felt good, she worked off her excess energy by shopping for things she didn't need.

When she felt bad she lingered in bed. On those days I could no longer make her laugh, which made me sad.

The mothers of my friends didn't stay in bed all day, so I tried to think of things Momma would like to do.

At my encouragement she renewed her memberships in the Literary Society and the Garden Club, then prevailed on me to speak in her stead when her turn to present the program rolled around. I reviewed a novel I thought the members might enjoy.

Had we realized that in her search for meaning in life Momma was filling her time with activities no longer of interest to her, we might have been more help.

She lost the joy of going to the movies or in visiting relatives, was frequently irritable, and picked fights with her friends and close family.

She would shut Daddy out of their bedroom for weeks at a time. He got so used to sleeping on the sofa he didn't seem to mind being in Momma's dog house. She'd send us to ask him a question and order us to bring back his reply. We all walked on eggs in our effort to keep the peace.

Nothing helped. We became experts at deception, keeping quiet about her problems when visitors came. Had we known she needed medical help sooner, the right doctor might have been diagnosed her as bi-polar sooner, and prescribed a more appropriate treatment to relieve her suffering than nerve medicine.

Slowly, though, Momma became her old self. Nothing we could name brought about the change, it just happened. We all welcomed it.

# Chapter Fourteen

New Acquisitions and Family Friends
1945-1946

More than anything else on earth, I wanted a friendship ring like the girls at church wore. Loretta Sansing's ring had a pretty blue stone set in gold. The stone caught the sun streaming through the church window and projected colorful rainbows on the wall.

All through the preacher's sermon I'd watch that ring on Loretta's slender finger and wonder, *Why not me?*

Why couldn't I have a ring like my friend's?

But Loretta didn't live in the country and didn't like to dirty her hands. I'd never be able to keep a ring like hers looking nice. Even though the stone in her ring matched my blue eyes, I had my heart set on a friendship ring, the kind my friend Sydney Anne Ball received for her birthday. Her shiny, wide band of silver had two little dangling hearts.

Yes, that was the kind of ring I wanted.

Way before Thanksgiving I found a picture of the ring in a newspaper ad, cut it out, and started dropping hints around our house.

That newspaper clipping never left my purse, and I slept with my purse under my pillow to make sure I'd dream about that ring.

Christmas morning finally arrived, and to my delight in the toe of my stocking, I found a small ring box. Not daring to hope, I carefully opened the box.

The ring inside was nothing like the picture I kept in my purse. It was even better than I'd hoped it would be. The silver hearts jingled every time my hand moved. The silver flashed in the sunlight, so bright it hurt my eyes.

I loved the way the ring looked on my finger. Unable to believe my good fortune, I spent the morning admiring it. I couldn't wait to show it off when our relatives came for the feast.

They arrived by threes and fours, bringing presents for us and their contributions to the meal. I hurried each of my cousins out to the swing where I first showed off my pretty ring, then pushed each one in the rope swing.

My ring finger soon began to hurt. When I checked to see why, I saw a blister forming at the base of my finger. That blister really hurt, so I slipped off my ring and carefully placed it in the small, dirt-filled circle formed by the nearest tree roots, where I could easily find it when I was ready to put the ring back on.

My cousin Donald Bailey soon complained that he was "tired of doing girl stuff". He wanted to go over on the school grounds and do boy things.

I led the way to the chin-up bar and Donald showed off on it for us until Ann called everybody in to eat.

After dinner Diane and I took turns washing dishes, then dried our hands. That's when I missed my ring. "Come on," I told Diane and headed out the front door. I ran up the slight grade, Diane right on my heels.

"Where are you going?" she asked, out of breath.

"You'll see." I stopped at the tree that supported the kids' swing and dropped to my knees on the ground. "Huh!"

"Well?" Diane asked.

"It's gone. The ring I got for Christmas is gone. Who could have taken it?"

I felt around all the tree roots, looked under those that did not touch the ground. My ring was nowhere to be found.

"Momma is going to kill me," I whispered under my breath. "I just got my ring this morning, and now it's gone." I refused to cry. Someone was bound to notice my eyes were red and then I'd have to confess.

How could I have been so careless? Was I jinxed when it came to rings?

When the company left, I searched under the tree again.

How could I tell my parents I'd already lost my precious gift? After what had happened to my other ring, Momma would be really disappointed in me. We both had thought I was mature enough now to keep up with jewelry.

I didn't sleep well that night and the next morning I crept outside before breakfast to search for the ring again. What had I hoped, that the fairies had brought it back?

When I still couldn't find the ring, I gave up and went in to eat. I slumped in my seat, knowing I'd soon have to confess my loss. And there, on the table in my empty cereal bowl, sat my ring.

Lesson learned.

I didn't take my ring off again until I outgrew it. I never knew who found that lost ring, but suspect it was my sister Ann. She's the only one in our household who would have taken it straight to Momma instead of giving it back to me.

In one of the first steps in his barn conversion, Daddy removed the hook for hoisting bales of hay into the loft and installed a floor-to-ceiling window sash in the opening where the hook had hung. The upstairs bedroom addition on the back of the house had a huge window exhaust fan used to pull the hot air out of the upstairs.

For a while after he returned home Little Robert apprenticed to become an electrician and occupied this room. He and Daddy regularly brought home discards from their remodeling jobs, nicer decorative things than those we had. Most often these were Victorian light fixtures or hand painted frosted glass globes suitable for the front porch lighting, things Momma treasured and for which I had no use.

One day, however, I got lucky. My brother brought home some bookcases and a truckload of hardback novels to fill the shelves. Wonderful books. I'd always loved to read, had even arranged a library of sorts in the attic surrounding the attic stairwell.

Little Robert's books joined mine. Some were adult fiction, most of which I read. One in particular, "The Turquoise," stands out in my memory. I'm certain I didn't understand everything on those pages, but that book was my introduction to romance.

Bless his heart, my brother questioned my parents about the advisability of allowing me to read the books, but nobody told me I couldn't. Juanita still occupied the front room, and my bed was in the middle of the attic, in a space without windows and walled in by my library shelves. I could read until late at night without anyone noticing or complaining, and frequently did.

Mrs. Hines arranged a surprise for me one time when I spent a week with them. She introduced Momma to a neighbor who had a litter of white Persian kittens. I'd spent most of my visit at that lady's house, playing with her kittens, and Mrs. Hines talked Momma into buying one for me.

Momma did, and when I went home, the kitten I'd named Honey rode home in my lap. With freedom to roam our house and enjoy the yard, she grew into a show-stopping cat with long white fur and green eyes.

One of my winter chores was bringing in coal for the coal stove that heated our house at that time. Honey loved to play in the coal pile and would come inside absolutely filthy, so that most of the time she had dingy gray fur. On the day before we were to have a party I'd give Honey a bath. She never learned to like water, but afterwards she knew she looked pretty, and would stretch out on the coffee table and preen.

One time we wanted her to look especially pretty and put bluing in her bath. The thick long fur along her back turned green. Certain Momma would kill us, we added bleach to the rinse water. Honey turned yellow, preferable to green.

When she was old enough, we bred Honey to a friend's male Persian cat. By mid- summer, she grew so heavy with kittens we felt guilty for causing her such misery. She'd lie for hours in the sunshine on the porch and I'd watch for hours, fascinated by the way her big belly quivered and jumped.

One day Momma said, "Honey's time is nearing," so I spread a soft blanket in a cardboard box beside my bed. Honey had a mind of her own.

When I came home from school the next afternoon, Momma took me upstairs to see my proud cat, the mother of six tiny kittens with tightly closed eyes, frantically nursing.

Honey had dropped her kittens in the middle of my bed while I was at school.

One kitten was solid black. I promised it to my uncle Ralph.

If they came to visit during canning season, Grace Hines would ask for a peeler and peel apples, a diamond sparkling on every finger as she helped.

When Jim and Suzie had a litter of puppies, I let Mr. Hines choose one.

Jim, our fox terrier, had a little stump for a tail, which is common for the breed, so Daddy decided he should cut off each puppy's tail.

He should have called us to help him. Perhaps he suspected none of his offspring had the stomach for the job, for he tried to hold a puppy in one hand, a hatchet in the other, then hack off the tail. He cut the first one off too short, then grew cautious and each tail that followed was left progressively longer, until the sixth puppy barely had the tip of its tail chopped off.

It took those tiny nubs several weeks to heel and until they did, whenever a puppy tried to sit down, it yelped. Daddy felt really bad, and all the puppies Suzie birthed were allowed to keep their tails.

Mrs. Hines named their puppy with the three-inch stump for a tail, Happy, and each summer when I went for my week-long visit, I'd take Happy for daily walks. He liked to walk down Twentieth Street, which ran behind the Hines' house to the drug store at the bottom of the hill, where I'd buy each of us an ice cream cone. Happy loved ice cream.

The rest of my visit I spent reading Mrs. Hines' books and Mr. Hines' *Esquire* magazine. She later told me she worried about what I might be reading in a man's magazine. I told her I liked the poetry. Things like:

"I eat honey on my peas,
I've done it all my life.
Course it makes the peas taste funny,
But it keeps 'em on the knife."

Their Victorian house had back stairs the servants used and wide front stairs leading to landing story with lots of nooks and crannies for me to explore before reaching the second floor. The maid wore crisp white uniforms and smiled at me a lot. She lived in a little cottage out back by the dog's run.

Before going there for my first stay Momma had lectured me on how to be a proper guest. She warned I would be considered impolite if I didn't eat everything on my plate. There weren't many foods I didn't like, and figured I'd have no problem cleaning my plate, but I'd never come face to face with wilted lettuce before.

Mr. Hines had a well-kept garden where he proudly picked fresh vegetables every day for us to eat. The first night, the maid prepared wilted lettuce and set a large platter of it in front of me.

"We just love wilted lettuce," Mrs. Hines said, half-way through the meal. "What about you?"

*Hot bacon grease poured over fresh leaves of green lettuce is a fine way to ruin good lettuce,* I longed to say. Instead, I smiled politely and said, "It's good."

So, the maid made a point of serving wilted lettuce every night, sometimes for lunch, too.

For the week I spent under their roof each summer I got to pretend I was the only child of rich parents who treasured me for my brains. I wasn't just another pair of hands to help weed the garden and can.

When I returned home, I began publishing a newspaper in my cozy upstairs room. Our portable typewriter clicked and clacked late into the night. I produced the first issue, then typed copies of those two pages three more times, and on Sunday morning at Sunday School, distributed my newspaper to my girlfriends.

Instead of listening to our teacher's lesson, Janet, Loretta and Sydney Ann read my paper.

Word of that got back to Daddy, but he just laughed.

I represented my school in the County Spelling Bee, was awarded a medal from the American Legion, was named Valedictorian of my class, and had been nominated by my teachers for a nationwide talent hunt. Nothing ever came of it. I think it was a scam to attract wealthy parents interested in furthering their child's education with classes in acting and ballet.

Nine of us students completed seventh grade and graduated from Hall Kent School. Most would go on to Shades Cahaba High School. I would enroll in Edgewood School for eighth grade. Mrs. Jones took me aside after graduation and told me, "You've been a big fish in a little pond in this school. I doubt you'll even be noticed at Edgewood and for sure not in high school, so don't expect too much."

I left Hall Kent with mixed emotions. I'd heard my first dirty jokes on the playground and had laughed, unwilling to admit I was so young and innocent I didn't understand the jokes.

My friends at church came from families far better off than mine and I felt certain their school friends were of equal rank in the community. It had never occurred to me that I would again be at the bottom of the pile and need to fight my way back up.

What if the other students didn't like me? What if they were smarter?

*What if they weren't?* I silently questioned, feeling better.

Mrs. J might be in for a surprise.

After ignoring my pleas for years, my parents bought a used piano, an old black upright delivered by two dark-skinned men in a black truck, and the summer passed so quickly I didn't find time to worry.

Although it was the ugliest piano I'd ever seen, and badly need turning, I was thrilled every time I walked through our now crowded living room and saw it sitting there. I started piano lessons right away, studying from *Teaching Little Fingers To Play*, with Miss Abbott, who taught my friends, and Momma moved the horsehair sofa out to the screened in porch to relieve the overcrowding in the living room.

I quickly progressed right through the book, proudly earning gold stars like all beginning students and, at the end of the summer, played in my first recital.

My knees shook so badly I could hardly walk out on stage in my tacky yellow taffeta gown with the brown trim. I took my seat and arranged my shaking hands on the keys. It required two attempts to find the right keys and play them in the correct order. I was one of the oldest performers, but played a beginner's tune.

Momma always insisted I willingly play for her guests when asked, so playing for an audience didn't bother me. Playing before an experienced audience of piano students and their families gave me pause.

My sisters had no interest in taking eight-dollars-a-month lessons, although Juanita let me teach her a little of what I'd learned. Sometimes, before I left for my lesson on the first Saturday of the month, Momma and Daddy would have a scavenger hunt to find enough money to cover Miss Abbott's bill.

I filled the rest of the summer with Vacation Bible School, Girl's Auxiliary camp and weeding the flowerbeds. Momma would loosen the dirt around each plant, then I'd move in. On my knees my job was to ferret out every tiny root and dried runner of Bermuda grass.

"You'll have to dig deeper than you think to find all the roots," Momma repeated so often I adopted 'dig deeper' as my personal motto because if I missed a tiny root or dead-looking runner, new sprigs of Bermuda grew back within a week and I had the job to do all over again.

I became a true believer in Momma's catch phrase, applied her advice to other parts of my life, determined to dig deeper in everything I did. If a subject in class interested me, I looked it up in the school library and check out a book on the subject or question my teacher until I was satisfied I understood the answers. Then I'd tuck the new-found knowledge away in my growing brain, certain I'd find need for that particular bit of information at some future time in my life.

I especially liked to read biographies of famous people like Paul Revere and Johnnie Tremain, and of baseball players like Ty Cobb and Satchel Page.

The prior fall Momma had purchased special outfits for my sisters to wear on dates, pleated plaid skirts with matching sweaters. One outfit was predominantly blue, the other brown. I was not old enough to date, and was brokenhearted that I didn't get a pretty, new outfit like theirs.

I especially coveted the blue one. By the time I was old enough to date, matching ensembles were no longer in vogue. Never a stickler for fashion, I'd have worn their matching ensembles anyway, but my sisters never outgrew their pleated skirts, so I didn't inherit either of those pretty outfit.

Finally, school started. I enrolled in Edgewood School and rode my bike those three miles to get there, even on rainy mornings when I'd arrive with my clothes dripping wet. At that time, the hems of girl's skirts fell just below the knees, the perfect length to get caught in my bicycle spokes.

The school bus passed me every morning on Oxmoor Road pedaling my way to school. My Hall Kent friends from prior years would beat the side of the bus and wave to me.

My girlfriends from church and a few of their school friends had formed a friendship club for girls and invited me to join. Every Monday afternoon we met in a different home. Our weekly agenda: discussions of our latest heartthrobs and the next party we planned to give.

We decided on an afterschool party. I offered my house, where we'd have plenty of fun things to do. We six girls could only think of five boys to invite, but to our delight, all five promised to come.

For most of the afternoon we rode Daddy's cable car swing. He and Little Robert had strung the swing purely for our pleasure, and at the Training Union parties given at our house it had quickly become a big hit.

A thick, strong cable stretched between two tall trees about fifty yards apart in our front yard. The cable ran through a pulley that supported a swing seat wide enough for two, launched from a platform at the top of the hill in our front yard.

At the bottom of the hill, a knot in the cable stopped the swing with a sudden jolt that shook the tree. The knot kept the riders from crashing into it. The sudden stop sent the swing and its riders up in the air in a wide arc.

It took some adjusting the first time to assure the riders wouldn't hit the tree, but once Daddy had the conveyance safe and working just right. We spent many enjoyable hours at family gatherings and church parties operating the swing for our guests. As a safety measure between parties Daddy locked the swing to the upper platform.

On Wednesdays I took my roller skates to school in my bicycle basket and wore the hard-sole shoes my skates clamp on because after school I'd leave my bike at Janet's, and we'd go roller skating. Our favorite street, one that looped up and back down a steep hill happened to be where. Billy Watkins, Billy Walker, and Janet's heartthrob Lawrence Harrison all lived. If we were lucky one or more of them would be out as we skated by.

Their street was a favorite of skaters, especially those of us who threw caution to the wind and raced down their hill. There was no way to stop at the bottom short of crashing on someone's lawn, so we'd raced out into the busy street, me with my eyes closed. My parents never knew how close I came to breaking my neck or getting hit by a passing car.

Yes, I discovered boys that year, and, thanks to Billy Watkins, enjoyed my first taste of bubble gum. Billy was a cute, but immature boy in my class. He gave me a ring from a box of Cracker Jacks and I faithfully wore it and my friendship ring. Over Christmas vacation Billy's mother drove him down to my house to deliver a gift to me, three flat slabs of bubble gum, each packaged with a baseball card.

Since it had been impossible to buy bubble gum during the war, I had never sampled it and suspected I hadn't missed much, but he seemed tickled to be bringing me bubble gum, so I pretended I was thrilled.

After he left I tried a piece and discovered the chewy stuff took some getting used to. It made my teeth hurt, my jaws ache, and was also hard on my hair, for my long strands would blow across the sticky bubbles I blew and get stuck.

Billy called me later and invited me to go to Sally DeLay's holiday dance with him. The eighth graders had all attended private, after-school dance classes in Mountain Brook in sixth grade. Those same students were now celebrating their birthdays by giving formal dances where they could put what they'd learned about proper deportment to the test. I had not attended those classes and had no idea what was expected of me at this dance.

Momma changed the color of the ribbons on my second-hand yellow taffeta dress and I curled my hair on socks.

A date for these parties meant the boy's mother drove him to my house, where he'd knock on our front door and help me into the back seat of their car. He'd climb in beside me and I'd try to think of something witty to say. I'd end up conversing with his parent during the long ride to the rented dance studio in Mountain Brook. The back seat of a mid-forties model Buick or Oldsmobile seemed huge to me and I always felt ill at ease sitting beside a boy in the dark.

Once Billy and I joined the other guests in the dimly lit hall, a little of my nervousness eased. If I did something stupid, who would see? Crepe paper hung from the ceiling, and while I was admiring it Sally, my hostess, tied a dance card on my wrist.

David Pruitt and his nerdy friends began signing their name to my dance card. It was soon filled, but not by the boys with whom I'd hoped to dance.

My dancing ability was questionable at best. When Ann and Juanita were learning ball room dancing in our living room, I'd had to take the boy's part, leading them around the floor. Now I had to constantly remind myself I was not to lead. I hadn't had the benefit of dancing classes and my first dance with anyone was always a battle of wills.

My partner seemed nervous, and could have attributed my missteps to the newness of wearing a long skirt. Instead, he apologized repeatedly.

Then I danced with Billy.

Bless his heart. I wouldn't have been at the dance if not for him, but I felt mature beyond my years, and dancing with Billy like dancing with a little brother, if I'd had one. I kept glancing around, hoping no one saw me with him.

The punch and cookies were probably the best part of the evening, and then it was time for the last dance. With Billy. I enjoyed this one a little more, for who knew when I'd get to step out like Cinderella again? I tried to store a mental image of the dancing couples in the dimly lit room and keep for all time.

When school resumed after the holidays I discovered I'd left an orange in my locker for those two long weeks and it had spoiled. The putrid odor refused to dissipate and I had to move my books to another locker. To this day I can't stand the smell of moldy citrus fruit.

On Valentine's Day, Billy Walker, a boy in the other eighth grade class, gave me an unexpected Valentine. He'd changed the inside words from "I *like* you very much," to "I *love* you very much," and showed it to all his friends before handing it to me in the hall. At the time, I barely knew his name.

At recess not long after, he asked me to wear his Boy Scout ring. Although he was no taller than me, he had short thick fingers, so I wore his ring on a chain around my neck, the ring Billy Watkins gave me still on my finger. The two Billy's had grown up together and maybe it was only natural they'd both like the same girl.

Billy Walker invited me to his birthday dance, and later to a party his Boy Scout troop planned. As luck would have it, David Pruitt, a nerdy classmate, asked me first. I didn't get that many party invitations and thought the party might be fun. David sounded so hopeful, I found it hard to say no to him, especially after Daddy gave his permission for me to go, so I told David, "Yes."

I hung up and the phone rang again: Billy Walker was calling to invite me to the same event.

Hoping I could somehow get out of my promise to David, I delayed the inevitable by telling Billy I'd have to ask my father and would let him know the next day.

I told Daddy, "I've been invited to go to the same party by a second boy, one I'd much rather go with."

He said, "That's too bad, but you can't break your date with David to go to the same party with another boy. You either go with David, or you stay home."

*Shoot!*

For an instant I seriously considered staying home, because now that I was forced to go with David, the party wouldn't be as much fun, but it would get me out of the house. How bad could an evening with David be?

Next day, it nearly broke my heart to admit to Billy I'd accepted David's invitation first, and would have to go with him even though I'd rather not.

Like a true gentleman Billy said he understood and would see me there.

The night of the party Daddy went over a short list of does and don'ts before David arrived. Things like, "Don't let me find out you let that Walker boy monopolize your time."

Daddy would have been proud of me. Billy and I played one game of ping pong and twice I danced with him. David monopolized the rest of my time. I've sometimes wondered if the two of them ever discussed me, but I think not.

Billy was too well bred, and David acted like he knew he was stretching his luck, getting to take me out.

The unpopular girls gave parties in their living rooms and invited me to some of those. We played spin the bottle. If the bottle pointed to me I was expected to go outside with the boy who had made the bottle spin and stand still while he kissed me. A cold kiss? Eeewww! Who made up those rules?

Spring came, and with it the annual County-wide spelling bee. Janet Landers had won it the year I'd represented Hall Kent, so I thought, *Why not me this year?* We shared the same classroom. I'd learned the same new words she had and had studied long lists of words late into the night.

She beat me again. Just plain out-spelled me to earn the honor of representing Edgewood School in the County championship, which she won and went on to compete in the State.

I'd lost, a four-letter word I discovered I didn't like hearing.

Right before the end of school, Ann had emergency surgery for an ovarian cyst and while she was recuperating downstairs in Momma's big bed, I invited Janet and her baby brother to visit her. He was so funny he made Ann laugh, which hurt her so badly she asked them to leave.

Suddenly it was the week before graduation, a week filled with parties and fun. One afternoon we had a trolley party to Bessemer and back on a chartered bus. Trolleys didn't run where we wanted to go. Just the week before Billy Walker had asked for his ring back and promptly gave it to Sally Delay. On the bus she went out of her way to show me his ring fit her finger just fine.

I had a miserable time.

Next day, the parents hosted a barbeque and swimming party. I spent the whole afternoon trying to get my memory book signed without getting it wet.

I wore a new dress for graduation, "The kind a grownup young lady about to enter high school should wear," Momma said.

The only things I had to look forward to over the Summer were my piano lessons and church camp. I'd have to endure the long, hot Summer without my closest friends, the teachers at Edgewood School who'd shared their knowledge with me, while keeping me in line. They'd tried hard to prepare me for high school.

I didn't like having the whole Summer to worry about whether or not they'd done a good job.

# Chapter Fifteen

The Church Swimming Party
1947

On Sunday nights at Training Union, Mrs. Austin taught my class of twelve-year-olds, Mr. Austin those already thirteen. After numerous failed attempts, we girls finally convinced our leaders to chaperone a joint swimming party for us to be held at Robinwood Plunge on a hot Saturday afternoon in July.

The pool was in a city park located in West Birmingham and since Baptist boys and girls didn't usually swim at the same time, this would be our big chance.

Janet Johnson, Loretta Sansing and Harriet House were my best church friends at that time. For weeks ahead we talked on the phone of nothing but that momentous event. All three towered above me and liked to tease me about never having grown up.

My friends and I were excited about the party because the thirteen-year-old boys were included, boys far more mature than the ones we had attended Church with for years. Those older boys had already completed a year of high school. Some of them attended the big downtown schools.

We'd set our sights on the older of two brothers whose family had moved to Mountain Brook and joined our church in the last year. Bobby, the brother our age, was okay, but his voice hadn't changed yet. His brother Harold's had. He was really, really cute, with dark, unruly hair and mischievous eyes, but seemed totally unaware every teenage girl at church had a crush on him.

Since we were to play games at the park and eat before swimming, I wore my new playsuit with elastic in the legs and carried my bathing suit and towel in a drawstring bag. I wanted to look good, even if my hair was wet, so I packed my hair brush, too. A wise girl didn't go anywhere without a hair brush.

When we arrived at our destination, we all felt awkward and formed two self-conscious groups determined by sex. The girls, in twos and threes, whispered behind their hands. The boys quickly formed a large circle, their backs to us and their voices loud.

Mr. Austin suggested we play softball to break the ice.

Even the game didn't really help the two groups mix. Mr. Austin named two of the boys team captains, although it was widely known Janet could outhit any boy and I could run really fast.

The captains chose sides and we played three innings, just long enough to show the boys I could hit the ball out of the infield but couldn't field the ball. When I saw a line drive coming my way, I'd shut my eyes and pray I wouldn't miss it. As luck would have it, I did. Then a runner charged me at third base and made me drop a fly ball.

I was a pretty good batter for my size. The boys never expected it. When my turn at the plate came, they would motion to each other to move up. I'd smack the ball right between second base and the short stop, run to first base and sometimes even to second before stopping to catch my breath and watch them scurrying after my line drive.

At the picnic following the ball game, we stuffed ourselves on fried chicken, potato salad and watermelon. "You'll have to wait for your food to digest before you change into your swimsuits," Mr. Austin said.

Loudly complaining, we got back into boy/girl groups to pass the time. The boys sprawled beneath a tree. The girls preened at a picnic table where we were sure to be seen and giggled behind our hands.

When I walked to the trash can, I could feel those masculine eyes on me and, on the way back, ran my brush through my long, blonde hair.

I'd had such success attracting the boys' attention, each of my friends took a stroll.

Then Mr. Austin called us to gather around and asked, "Can all of you swim?"

Once or twice each summer I'd meet my friends at Hollywood Country Club and spend the day in the Club's public pool, a five-mile bike ride along a busy highway each way. Momma insisted at least one sister ride along with me, so I didn't get to go as often as I'd like. I hadn't been swimming enough to master breathing with my strokes.

To make matters worse, I couldn't float. Janet had tried to teach me to float. Told me to lie back in the water and just relax. That she'd catch me if I started to sink.

I always did. I had small bones and no fat, nothing to keep me afloat, so I sank. I'd learned to hold my breath forever, and do the breast stroke across the deep end of the pool before coming up for air. I felt comfortable at the bottom of the pool, where I would hold my breath for a long, long time and listen to the sound of the bubbles escaping from my bathing cap. Sometimes I'd pretend I was a deep-sea diver searching the bottom for pearls.

It took all my will to keep from telling Mr. Austin I couldn't swim. If I did, I'd be relegated to the little kids' end of the pool, not the best place for me to attract Harold or one of the other boys, so I kept quiet.

When no hands went up, Mr. Austin said, "Good," and rattled off a list of rules, then sent us to get dressed. The strong smell of bleach in the girl's dressing room burned our noses, so we hurriedly pulled on our bathing suits and checked each other to make sure or sits fitted right. We'd never have lived it down if a something slipped and exposed too much skin.

When all our suits were snugly tied, we strolled out single file, feeling exposed and suddenly shy again.

The boys were already in the pool watching—we hoped—as we sidled past to arrange our neatly folded towels and hair brushes on a bench.

For a while, we girls just sat on the edge of the pool watching the boys do cannonballs all around us and splash water in our eyes. Then

Janet slid into the water and ducked her head to wet her long hair. It floated out behind her.

"Come on in. The water feels good," she said.

Harriet and Loretta held hands as they stepped off the last step and water crept up to their waists. I couldn't stand to get wet gradually.

I asked Janet to stand under the end of the diving board and show me how deep the pool was there. I always sank, but if I jumped in with enough force to kick off the bottom I'd pop right back up to the surface like a cork, and if I was lucky eyes would no longer be trained on me as I dog paddled over to the side.

Where Janet stood, the water only came up to her chest.

I usually walk out to the end of the diving board and jump in, feet first. I didn't want the boys to see that I couldn't really swim and for a while I sat on the side dangling my feet, waiting for their attention to be on someone else.

Then somebody called me chicken. That's all it took. I marched right out to the end of the board, too self-conscious to take a good bounce and simply stepped off, my arms at my sides.

I sank toward the bottom of the pool without much force.

*Why hadn't I jumped?* I was taking far too long to reach the bottom and when I did, the bottom felt uneven, the water much deeper than I'd thought.

Was Janet that much taller than me?

I kicked off the bottom, but not as hard as I intended. Only one of my hands broke the surface of the water, not my face. I promptly sank again.

What a silly fool I'd been, all because I hadn't wanted the boys watching me jump in. Now I wished they were watching. I was in real trouble. With my feet unable to touch the bottom, I had no way to push off. No way to shoot back up to the surface and suck eeded air into my lungs.

Desperate, I kicked up, hard, failed to break the surface and began to sink again. Bubbles rose all around me. Just over my head was a bright red ball. I tried to wrap my arms around it. I only missed it by inches and started to sink again.

This time I kicked really hard, got one hand out of the water, made what seemed to me like a big splash, but slowly lost what ground I'd gained and began to sink once more.

The harder I tried to reach the surface, the deeper I sank.

Next time around I finally broke out of the water and opened my mouth to yell. Too late. I swallowed a mouth full of water and went under again. Air escaped from my bathing cap in a diminishing stream of tiny bubbles.

The weight of the water pressed me down, down, down, until I settled on the bottom while up at the surface, legs, some thin and some long, performed a graceful water ballet. The bright light up there hurt my eyes. The fight went out of me.

As I sank, bits of conversation came to me, and laughter.

*Would I ever have cause to laugh again?*

*Hey, can't you see someone's dying down here?* I wanted to yell, wishing I could safely be back up there with my friends. I'd never again be ashamed to cling to the side of the pool.

What if no one missed me until the party was over? My arms and legs no longer responded to my brain signals, so for me the party was nearly over.

What would Daddy say when nobody brought me home? Would he be mad at me, or at the Austins and my friends?

*This isn't their fault. I should never have stepped off that diving board.*

A single bubble escaped my cap and I squeezed my eyes shut to hold back my tears as the chlorine-laced water cradled me at the bottom of the pool, gently rocking me in the ghostly quiet.

Then Mr. Austin told Harold he'd seen my hand come out of the water and thought I might be in trouble.

"I am, I am," I tried to yell. Words wouldn't form.

I heard a splash, felt the slap of disturbed water, waited for the saving hands to take hold of me. Another splash, another jolt, and strong arms yanked me off the bottom and a hairy elbow forced its way beneath my chin. We sliced through the water as my rescuer easily dragged me up, up, up to the surface I had tried so hard to reach.

Rough hands pulled me out of Harold's arms and laid me face-down on the hard concrete. Someone hit me on the back, hard. *Ouch!*

"Nothing," a distraught male voice said.

"I'll try artificial respiration," whoever was kneeling over me said.

*Harold? How would I ever face him?*

He forced my shoulders down against the concrete, made my ribs hurt as he pressed hard on my back.

I heard every word spoken over me, about me. Felt the same frog in my throat Janet had in hers when she asked, "Did she drown?"

"I don't think she was under long enough for that," Mrs. Austin assured her in a shaky voice. "Was she?"

"Only a minute. Maybe a little more," Mr. Austin responded.

*A minute? Seemed like hours to me.*

Harold pressed on my back and counted, "One, two, three, four. Rest, two, three, four." And again.

Though I heard every word spoken, much as I wanted to, I couldn't respond, was unable to answer their questions. No matter how hard I tried I was unable to shout, *Don't give up on me. Not yet. Don't stop. I can hear you, and I don't want to be dead.*

Strange. For a moment I was floating up above them and looking down on their desperate attempt to save me beside the pool.

I prayed long and hard Harold would keep trying, wished I could tell Mr. Austin I wanted to live. My life was all still ahead of me. I'd only that year discovered boys and had so much still to learn.

*Don't stop, don't stop*, I kept thinking. *I still have my college years ahead of me.*

*There is so much I still wanted to do.*

*My life can't possibly be over. Daddy will miss me too much.*

*Why me, God? Have my sins finally caught up with me?*

"Breathe," Harold murmured above me.

I felt the urge.

And did.

Water gushed up and out, burning my throat and strangling me as I tried to gulp in air. I couldn't stop coughing, and began to cry at the same time.

Being able to feel again felt so good I didn't have it in me to complain, although my lungs were on fire.

I could breathe. *I've survived!*

I struggled to sit up.

Mrs. Austin wrapped me in a towel, and insisted I sit on the side of the pool for the rest of the party, with only my feet in the water. I had no one to talk to and nothing to do while sitting there, but relive what had happened to me.

Mr. Austin reported my near-death experience to Daddy, who then calmly laid down the law. No more stepping off the thirty-foot diving tower at the Country Club. No more pretending I could swim when I couldn't. He never mentioned swimming lessons, but he did say, "I hope next time you'll think before you leap."

His lecture found a receptive chord in my brain. I'd faced a life-changing moment and survived.

*Good job*, I thought, and thanked my lucky stars.

# Chapter Sixteen

A Family's Loss

For Momma's sister, my Aunt Edith, her husband, Uncle Bernie, and their daughter, Diane, losing their five-year-old son Freddie to cancer truly was the end of life as they'd known it. The rest of us didn't realize until later they'd buried any hope for future happiness along with their son.

His death started a slowly revolving tornado of events that sucked his loved ones into its vortex. Until then, their little family had faithfully attended Church with us, silently praying for Freddie.

Afterwards, my aunt and uncle turned away from God, saying no merciful Father would allow their son to suffer the way Freddie had.

Or let their son die.

As I grew older, I looked forward to seeing Aunt Edith and Uncle Bernie at family gatherings, not just Diane, although she was the nearest of my cousins to my age. Artificially cheerful greetings were my aunt and uncle's specialty, their false gaiety attributed to holiday open houses they dropped by, before coming to our house for the family gathering.

My parents no longer went out for fun, not even on New Year's Eve. Momma's long, iridescent taffeta dress with the wide, full skirt forlornly hung in the back of her closet, a faded reminder of times past. Seeing Aunt Edith and Uncle Bernie so carefree made me wish my parents partied, too.

With only a little encouragement Aunt Edith would shrug her shoulders and do the Charleston at family gatherings. Or sing "Hold That Tiger" with Uncle Bernie. Or the two of them would dance the Bunny Hug. I longed for my staid parents to become the life of the party, but deacons in the Baptist Church didn't dance or drink.

Although Diane's pre-teen eyes sometimes revealed pain or hinted at shame, I never dreamed her parents were the cause. She and I would sneak away from the others, find a quiet corner and discuss the books we'd recently read, talk about the new ones received as gifts, and confess how anxious we were for the gathering to be over so she could go home and curl up with a book.

When Diane was about twelve and living in East Lake, a side ache sent her to the hospital. "A possible appendicitis," Momma said.

When Diane came home from the hospital, Aunt Edith invited me over to spend the weekend with them.

Huddled beneath the covers in the privacy of her room late that first night Diane confided, "I wish I had died instead of Freddie. If I had, my family would still be happy."

I had no idea what to say.

"The doctor didn't remove my appendix," she whispered. "I was punched hard in the stomach. That's what sent me to the emergency room."

For a long moment a stealth noise in the next room silenced her.

I didn't know what to do, other than to just be there for her. She was crying softly. Tears streamed down her cheeks and she buried her face in a pillow.

The two of us read together a lot that weekend. Diane liked to read a page, then close her book. After watching her do this several times, I asked, "Why do you do that?"

I like to guess what will happen on the next page, then read more and see if I'm right."

Was she fantasizing? Had she found a way to escape the harsh reality of her life? I suppose that's why everyone reads, but I suspected Diane's reading brought her more satisfaction than most readers enjoyed.

Later, from whispered conversations between relatives, comments not intended for my ears, I learned that in a drunken rage Uncle Bernie had hit her.

I spent some happy times with her family, too, like the week I spent with them in a cabin on Guntersville Lake, where Uncle Bernie was remodeling the weekend home of his boss. I only saw my uncle at night, when the four of us played canasta after dinner and ate little fish called sardines jammed together in a funny-shaped flat can. I finally took the risk and ate the tiny bones the way Aunt Edith insisted.

One day Diane and I set out in inner tubes to float on the calm, wide lake. The gentle breeze at our backs kept us moving at a lovely, leisurely pace. All we had to worry about was keeping the cabin in sight, my aunt's one rule.

Away from the ever-watchful eyes and ears of my aunt we enjoyed the warm sun on our backs and lost all track of time. Engrossed in a discussion about the latest Laura Ingalls Wilder book, we floated much further than Aunt Edith said we could go.

I looked back over my shoulder and realized I could no longer make out the cabin, and suggested we paddle back the way we'd come.

We couldn't.

The wind was now on our backs, and a strong current tugged at my feet. We didn't have paddles, and we could not make any headway with just our hands and feet.

Suddenly a big motor launch came roaring up beside us, Aunt Edith at the wheel. We were exhausted, and delighted to see her. As she helped us over the side of the boat, she pointed out howclose near we'd floated to the dam. When she'd noticed the current taking us right to it, she'd jumped into the boat and raced after us.

Another half hour and I hate to think what would have become of the two of us. We stayed close to the cabin for the rest of the week.

Diane and I eventually grew apart. She lived across town and attended a city school, so we didn't see each other often, only on holidays.

Years later Uncle Bernie took a job in Florida, and while working down there, he committed suicide. His death turned out to be an eye opener for all of us, but not until Aunt Edith blew all the money she'd received from the sale of her house on a California vacation with friends, instead of learning to run a motel the way she'd planned. With no work experience or saleable skills, the penniless widow returned to Birmingham and her mother took her in.

By the time Momma Rosie realized her troubled daughter was an alcoholic, the damage to Aunt Edith's liver was irreversible, and in a few years cirrhosis of the liver ended her misery.

That's when the truth finally came out. All those years it was Edith who had a drinking problem. She'd had it for years. Not Bernie. Out of love for her, he had covered for his wife, shouldered all the blame for her actions, and silently suffered her abuse.

In an alcohol-induced rage it was Aunt Edith who punched Diane in the stomach, not Uncle Bernie.

*Never him.*

# Chapter Seventeen

Testing the Water
1947-1948

Daddy never took vacations, but he encouraged Momma to take us on trips. So, in late Summer of 1947, as Daddy liked to put it, he packed all his women folks off to the Baptist Conference Center in Ridgecrest, North Carolina, in Momma's new, maroon-colored Dodge, to attend Training Union Week.. Another young woman from church rode with us.

I loved North Carolina, the rugged green mountains and clear streams flowing over rocky stream beds beside the highway.

One afternoon during our free time, Momma drove Ann and Juanita to Ashville, North Carolina to tour the Biltmore Estates. I begged off to go horseback riding. I'd always had a deep love for horses and rode whenever I got the chance, which was usually once each summer at church camp.

I'd come on this trip because the camp brochure promised two-hour trail rides and I'd brought enough babysitting money on the trip to take a trail ride every day but one, the day I accompanied my family to Chimney Rock. From the rock's dizzying height, it seemed as if I was on top of the world.

Ann and Gene Burton had fallen in love, and she kept his mailman in Oklahoma busy delivering her daily letters to him. She'd given Gene her Ridgecrest address and every afternoon she futilely checked the conference post office for mail. On our last day, while Momma was checking out of our hotel and the rest of us were loading the car for the trip home, Ann made a final trip to the post office. No letter had come for her, but she brought back a fat envelope addressed in pencil for me from Emmett Hatfield, Gertrude's brother.

He'd written to me the Summer before from Hatfield, Indiana, where he was visiting family. Before leaving on this trip, I'd jokingly given him my address, not really expecting him to write. He'd matured into a good looking ninth grader over the past year and I couldn't wait to read his letter, but didn't dare open it while jammed in the back seat between my two sisters.

When Momma finally stopped for a Coke I ripped open the envelope and started to read. Emmett's smoking hot words singed my fingertips.

He missed me.

He needed me.

He couldn't wait to kiss me.

*Oh, yeah? It was never gonna happen.*

Not with him.

I ended that romance in a hurry, by simply never riding my bike past Gertrude's house again, which freed up lots of my time, and I poured my energy into piano practice, doing scales and finger exercises to stretch my reach. My hands were so small I couldn't reach a full octave. I progressed through two more John Thompson instruction books before school started.

If my sisters were jealous that I played and they hadn't had the opportunity, neither of them complained. I taught Juanita to read music and to play 'Hiawatha's Song', which she often did.

The church choir went on vacation and Janet and I sang duets while the offering plates were passed for evening worship. I had the best voice in the family, but I was tone deaf without Janet's beautiful alto notes sung near my ear. Surprisingly, our voices harmonized beautifully.

I always sat by her in choir, which created a problem when her throat decided to growl, just like my stomach sometimes growled, only louder. She had no control over it, and when the growling started, it always cracked us up.

At the end of the Summer, I turned fourteen. I'd talked so much about getting a record player for my birthday my parents gave in to shut me up. Momma found a second-hand console that only played seventy-eights. It wore out long before my recordings of 'Near You' and 'Mule Train' wore out.

For the start of school, I got a red Swedish-knit sweater with piano keys across the shoulders and musical notes above the ribbing. I fell in love with my sweater, wore it to church Labor Day weekend, and insisted I wasn't hot.

The following Tuesday I started high school. Between classes, cheerleaders in the halls handed out announcements for cheerleader tryouts. I latched onto one.

When Daddy had taken me to football games the previous fall, I'd watched the cheerleader's antics instead of the game.

I had liked what I'd seen and wondered, *Hey, why not me?*

The following morning, I told Momma I'd be home late and stayed after school for cheerleader practice, to learn how to lead cheers. There were six openings on the squad.

Only six, and almost thirty hopefuls like me determined to learn the cheers.

Next day every muscle in my body ached, but I practiced that afternoon, too, then rode the city bus to the end of the line and walked uphill for most of the three miles home.

To my surprise and Daddy's consternation, on Friday at tryouts, my name was one of those called.

I'd won a place on the squad.

At the time. our football coach had a big say in cheerleader selection. I later learned that he wanted someone small enough to be tossed up in the air and caught by the male cheerleaders on the team. At eighty-five pounds, I filled the bill.

It didn't matter to me why I'd won. I was thrilled I'd made the team.

Daddy was appalled. No girl from Dawson Baptist Church had ever been on the cheerleader squad. Momma and my sisters convinced him that I'd be wearing tights under my gored uniform skirt, so no one would see my underwear. He didn't realize those red tights were intended to show. By the time he witnessed me turning cartwheels at the first game of the season he'd invested too much money in my uniform and didn't want his good money wasted.

Thanks to my antics as a cheerleader, I finally earned peer recognition. Whether because I formed the top of the cheerleader's pyramid or because I landed on my backside when some team member tossed me in the air, then failed to catch me, I was never out of the limelight for long.

Cheerleading finally earned me the attention I wanted. One weekend, the captain of the football team pulled up in our drive and invited me to the football team hayride. I'd never once heard his name, much less spoken to him, but he was blue-eyed and cute and I badly wanted to go to the party with him.

In my excitement over being asked, I forgot I wasn't allowed to car date until I was sixteen. It hadn't come up in a long time. I accepted his invitation without first asking Daddy. This caused a big uproar, because an eleventh- grader was much too old for me to go out with.

"Bad things happened on a hay rides," Momma claimed.

"What things?"

Momma wouldn't say.

Finally, because I'd already told him I could go, they agreed to let me.

The skies opened up the day of the hayride. My date showed up at my door again to tell me they'd cancelled the hayride. The disappointed team members and their dates were going to a movie that night, instead.

I'd learned my lesson and asked Charles to wait while I went inside and asked permission, knowing full well what the answer would be.

My parents said no, of course. Bad things happened at movies, too.

I had to go back out on the porch and tell him I couldn't go. I never spoke to him again, which was no big surprise since I'd stood up the most popular boy in school on a Saturday night.

About the same time Charles Hosier took a liking to me. He'd never seemed to notice me at Edgewood School, maybe because he was in the other eighth grade. That all changed when he placed a tarnished identification bracelet with a broken clasp in my hand as we passed each other in the high school hall.

Daddy fixed the clasp, and the nightly dip in soapy water while I did the dishes soon had the silver shiny as new.

Charles rode a motorbike to school.

After about a month, he asked for his bracelet back. The same day, I saw it proudly displayed on Bobbie Hyde's wrist.

I quickly realized high school subjects were not much harder than those we'd studied in eighth grade. Mrs. Stephens taught my freshman English class. Jimmy S, who promised to become a star running back on our football team, sat across from me, another Elemental school graduate who'd never before spoken to me.

One Friday, right before going in to take the weekly English test, Jimmy took me aside and said, "Look, I'm having some problems keeping my grades up and if I don't make a passing grade on today's test, Coach won't let me play tonight. You don't want me to be ineligible do you?"

"Of course not," I said, horrified at the idea. "The team needs you."

"Then you'll help me?"

"You don't have enough time for us to cram now."

"But when you finish the first page of the test, you could pass your answers to me. Just don't let Mrs. Stephens see."

"That's cheating," I whispered, appalled.

"I know, but it's the only way I'll get to play. If I fail this test I'll be benched. You don't want me sitting out the game, do you?" he said, prevailing on my school spirit when he saw I intended to refuse.

His importance to the whole team couldn't be ignored, so I reluctantly agreed to his plan.

The bell rang for class and I took my seat, amazed Jimmy had so easily snookered me into promising to do something I didn't want to do.

I was nearly through with the test when Jimmy taped me on the shoulder and I slipped the first of my answers to him.

Before I could pass him the second page, Mrs. Stephens stopped beside our desks. "I'll take those," she quietly said, collecting our tests. "And both of you get zeros for the week."

I always earned good marks, so one zero wouldn't hurt my grade, but I knew for certain I could kiss goodbye any hope of someday being tapped into the National Honor Society.

My teacher sponsored the group.

Luckily, my parents never found out about that cheating episode. As expected, at the game that night, Smiley remained on the bench.

Our team won anyway.

Early in October I attracted the attention of Billy Kincaid, a cornet player in the band. I liked him, too, and once or twice a week after school I'd help him fold the newspapers for his paper route, then ride double on his bicycle as he delivered them.

Sometimes I'd skip lunch and sit in on band practice. All the band members were clowns, a fun group to be around.

One day, the band director announced he needed someone who could read music to play the glockenspiel. Billy encouraged me to volunteer, which meant that right before halftime I had to run to the restroom across the field and change into my band uniform. I'd march out onto the field with the band, play the glockenspiel for the half-time show, then change, rush back to the sidelines, and resume my cheerleading duties.

The first time I marched on the field with the band I wore a black skirt. My legs were the only bare legs on the field, and everyone in the stands laughed. Before the next game the director provided uniform pants for me, the ones his chubby clarinet-playing son in the band had outgrown.

It rained hard right before the last game of the year and by the end of the first half the field looked like our pig pin. When I marched out on the field with the band at half-time, I stepped right out of my shoe.

Being in the band meant Billy and I shared a seat on the band bus going to and from all the out of town games and parades. I had a great time. Once, on a dare, I smoked a cigar on the way to a parade. I pretended to like it, but I only smoked on a dare.

I loved marching in the Christmas parades and afterwards, the bus rides home. Tired, but in good spirits, the band members goofed off. One time an oboist turned his oboe upside down and played a weird tune. Soon they were all playing, each of them a different song.

On the day school got out for Christmas, Bobby Rollins, a cute boy in my homeroom, surprised me with a special gift. His mother probably picked it out for him, but I loved the little black faille makeup case with its shiny gold clasp, and for many years used it for an evening bag.

I don't think I'd ever exchanged three words with him, but when we returned to school after the holidays, we started a friendship that lasted all through school.

Billy Kincaid invited me to the Christmas Eve service at his church and he and his parents picked me up. On the way I opened my gift from him, a gold necklace with a football charm, the perfect gift.

Ann was Daddy's favorite and several times during the holidays we put her up to asking him to take us to the movies. If anyone else asked he'd say, "No," but he seldom refused her requests.

Although she could twist Daddy around her little finger, I was the one my parents let get away with murder. Cute, smart, and Momma's baby, my sisters would grumble.

About that time my best friend Janet Johnson fell in love with Robert Hubbard, a tenth grader who rode my bus to school, and she called me one afternoon to tell me the bus driver had let her ride the entire bus route with Robert, instead of dropping her off as they went through Edgewood, the way he usually did. She'd ridden to the end of the line where Robert got off. The bus driver had let her off as he passed back through Edgewood on his way back to the high school where he parked the bus overnight. She and Robert were both good students, and well behaved. The driver obviously liked them, but it was unlawful for him to allow outsiders to ride his bus.

I couldn't get used to Janet having a steady boyfriend. I'd always been the one going to parties while she baby sat most weekends. Her parents gave her more freedom, even allowing her to ride to football games behind Robert on his motorcycle.

I wasn't permitted to go out with boys old enough to drive, was cautioned to stay out of their cars. Of course I found ways around this. One was to say I was babysitting, but to go out on a date instead. Janet and I had both advertised to baby sit and we received calls for more jobs that we could take. She sometimes referred her caller to me, and that's where I got the idea of saying I was sitting for one of Janet's customers when I was asked out on a date. My parents didn't know who I was sitting for, and wouldn't be able to check up on me. I never got caught.

The bus driver was a real character. All he had to do was glance in the rearview mirror and any bad behavior stopped. Tall and skinny, he looked about seventy-years-old. Arthritis kept his fingers permanently crimped as if he was still gripping the steering wheel long after he came down the bus isle to quiet some rowdy kid, each step slow and carefully thought out.

He'd slide first one hand along the steering wheel and then the other when he had to make a turn, never taking his hands off the wheel. In all the years I watched the bus come and go, he never missed a day of work, and the bus was only late twice, neither of those his fault. "Mechanical failure," he told us.

One morning when I boarded the bus the atmosphere seemed charged, the raucous laughter replaced by subdued murmuring, causing me to wonder what was up.

It didn't take me long to find out. At the blind train crossing near Spalding, the bus had nearly been hit by a train. The road makes a sharp horseshoe bend to the left, leaving just enough room for the driver to stop, then ease forward to see down the track. While our driver listened for an approaching train, the older students helped make sure the track was clear. Somehow that morning, everyone overlooked an oncoming freight. From what I was told, the bus barely made it across the tracks and the near miss just about scared the wits out of even the meanest boys.

Another time the bus was stopped where Oxmoor Road crossed Green Springs Highway, waiting for downhill traffic to clear so we could cross. Some mornings the bus was stopped there for quite a while.

The busy highway had a wide center divider, and if the traffic cleared on our side the driver would pull out to the divider and wait for traffic on the other side to clear before completing the crossing. On this particular morning the traffic on our side didn't clear, so our bus didn't move.

The car facing us on Oxmoor Road started across while an eighteen-wheeler plowed down the hill. From my front row seat, I could tell the driver wasn't going to make it across.

*Gun it*, I silently pleaded.

She didn't speed up, didn't even pause at the center divider. I sucked in a quick breath. She kept on coming, driving her car straight into the path of an oncoming truck headed right for her. She didn't have a chance.

When two warning blasts of his air horn didn't make her stop, the truck driver stomped his brakes. His load swayed, righted itself and swayed again, and I watched in horror as the back wheels of his tractor trailer slowly slid around and passed the front wheels of his truck. I could no longer see the car. Had she braked, too?

Perhaps I'd blinked.

The truck's air brakes let out a pained squeal, followed by a sickening crunch of metal as the trailer jackknifed, tipped over, and spilled its load almost in front of us. The crumpled trailer scraped along the pavement for a hundred feet or more before coming to a grinding halt.

I opened my eyes as the silence was broken by thirty stunned school kids all talking at once. I'd lost sight of the woman. Was her car pinned beneath his cab?

I stood up on shaky legs to get a better view and saw her car stopped a hundred yards down the highway, her front bumper knocked crooked and touching the pavement on one side.

I marveled at how quickly it happened. The truck driver had done everything he could to avoid the accident, but his trailer looked like a squashed tin can. He might have been killed. We could have been killed, if the jackknifed truck had slid in our direction instead of staying on the highway.

*Thank you, God.*

We stayed on the bus and waited for help to come. Soon two Highway Patrol cars pulled up, their colorful lights flashing. One put out warning flares while another climbed on the bus, asked our driver some questions, jotted down his answers, then asked my name and what I'd seen. After taking down the personal information from a few more students, he got off the bus and we continued on to school, arriving just before homeroom ended.

A few days later a man came to our house and took a deposition from me. I think he was hired by the woman's insurance company because he didn't like the answers I gave and I wasn't about to change my story to please him. She was totally at fault. I'd been crossing that highway in a car or school bus for six years or more, and while I might be young, even I knew better than to pull out in front of a truck with the right of way. She was clearly in the wrong and in my opinion should be hung out to dry for causing the accident, I told him. Maybe that's why I didn't get asked to testify if there was a trial.

I witnessed another automobile accident that made a big impression on me. One Sunday night when my sisters went to youth group after the evening worship and arranged for one of the older males in the group to take them home when the meeting ended, Momma talked Daddy into taking us to see *Leave Her to Heaven*.

She claimed everyone was talking about it. I didn't see what all the excitement was about, just that some pretty woman everyone considered wicked murdered Cornell Wilde at a secluded lake. I didn't like the woman.

Janet and I had a crush on Cornell Wilde.

We stepped out of the movie into a misty fog or light rain that had left the streets wet. Momma was still talking to Daddy about how terrible the woman in the movie behaved when we pulled up to a stop sign, and she signaled to turn left.

Boom!

Metal crunched. The tires squealed as our car lurched out into the intersection. Momma's feathered hat flew off. I closed my eyes, afraid to watch what might happen next.

Nothing did.

I opened my eyes. Steam seemed to be rising from every side of our car.

Nope, fog.

Momma's feathered hat, still caught by one hat pen, hung down her back.

I briefly wondered if God was punishing us for going to that wicked movie.

A burly black man tapped on Momma's window. "Is everybody all right?"

Daddy said, "Let me take care of this," and stepped out of the car.

"I hope he hasn't been drinking," Momma murmured.

He and Daddy quickly came to an understanding. The man knew his brakes were bad, and hadn't noticed our car was stopped until it was too late. He'd skidded on the wet street and plowed right into us, damaging Momma's trunk to the tune of three-hundred-dollars in repairs, Daddy later found out. The man gave Daddy enough cash to cover the repair and said he was eternally grateful Daddy hadn't involved the police.

Other than being inconvenienced while the family car was in the shop, we escaped with only stiff necks.

Not long afterwards I started lessons with my new piano teacher, a vivacious young Greek woman who taught piano in Five Points, south of downtown and five miles from our house. I rode the city bus to and from those lessons every Saturday morning.

Valentine's Day fell on Saturday that year, and when the bus taking me home from my lesson stopped in Homewood, Billy Kincaid boarded the bus. He came down the aisle wearing a grin nearly as big as he was, a yellow Whitman's Sampler tucked under his arm.

He gave me the candy, we chatted for a few more blocks, then he pulled the cord to notify the driver he wanted off at the next stop. He was my date for my sorority's Valentine Dance that evening and I hadn't expected to see him before his mother drove him to our house to pick me up.

Ann had belonged to Les Amies, a high school sorority and I had naturally been invited to join that fall after a series of rush parties and an overnight initiation meant to scare us pledges half to death. A social club for girls of similar means and interests, we spent most of our time raising money for the next big party on our calendar.

Billy looked so cute in his Sunday suit and bow tie at the Sweetheart's Banquet. I wore a made-over green formal of Ann's.

Before school let out for the summer Billy dumped me and made up with his previous girlfriend, a pattern that plagued me all through school. A steady breaking up with me when school let out was no big deal, though. I usually met someone at the pool to liven up my summer.

One year I had a crush on our newspaper boy. He was several years older, and every afternoon he gunned his motorcycle as he flew past our house. Right before time for him to come by, I'd put on clean shorts and a halter and go out to water the flowerbeds near the road. If he ever noticed me, he didn't let on

My parents never bought anything on time. Daddy's paychecks were too uncertain. So when we needed a new refrigerator, he borrowed three-hundred-fifty dollars from Juanita. She was saving her wages from Alabama Power and Light to enter nursing school, but before she could enroll at the Baptist Hospital School of Nursing she needed more science units to meet the entrance requirements. Like Little Robert, she had returned to my high school in the Fall to take biology and chemistry at the same time. She caught the school bus with me and stayed up all hours studying, motivated to make good grades this time around.

Little Robert was taking prerequisites for college, too. Each morning, he left home long before we did and drove his Model A roadster to school. Juanita's slow start in the morning had not changed and I often walked to the bus stop alone. If the bus driver saw her running to catch the bus he'd wait for her. About once a week she missed the bus, and would roust Momma from her warm bed to drive her to school.

Juanita's attention no longer wandered and she made good grades. Little Robert did too. It was strange, attending the same school they attended, sometimes passing them in the halls. Little Robert was always with Grace, his latest girlfriend, and on weekends took her to stock car races, drive-in movies and after school got out, the Starlight Opera. She loved the symphony and he came to love the divorced veteran's little boy.

Back then a divorce implied the woman had done something bad. Without even meeting her, Momma decided Robert's life would be ruined, although it was Grace who brought him back to God by interesting him in the mission work she did with the homeless. Momma made their lives miserable at every turn and the romance finally cooled.

Little Robert refused to stay home at night. He loved to roller skate and kept his shoe skates in his car. Sometime he took us with him to an indoor rink out past West End.

I loved to watch the mirrored lights rotate above Little Robert's head when the rink manager called for singles to skate. My brother gracefully skated backwards, did fancy dance steps on wheels, always took the center of the skating rink floor and showed off when the lights were dimmed, usually partnering with the cutest girl in the rink.

One night while skating, I fell approaching a curve and sprawled face down across the path of oncoming skaters who, unable to stop, ran into me from all sides. I lay there, afraid to move and cause someone else to fall, too stunned to get out of their way. Then a familiar pair of shoe skates skidded to a halt beside me and strong, welcome arms helped me to my feet.

Little Robert had noticed my plight and hurried to my side.

He drove a Model A convertible with a rumble seat and when my sisters got lucky, he gave them a ride home from school. Everyone loved to ride with him.

The school year passed quickly and my siblings went on to do other things. Juanita moved into the dormitory for nursing students, which they called the nurses' home, where evening curfew was observed and advance requests for weekend passes required.

In August of 1948 Ann married Gene Burton in a formal ceremony at Dawson church. Juanita served as maid-of-honor, Gene's sister Gwen and I were bridesmaids. We wore long gowns in pastel shades of taffeta and Bo Peep bonnets to match our gowns.

For me, all the wedding turmoil seemed like a lark until the preacher's final prayer, when it dawned on me Ann would be living with Gene and no longer making my clothes. Regret at my loss, not wedding sentiment, caused my sudden rush of tears.

Before the start of school for me, I spent my usual week with Grace and Elmer Hines. She'd cut the cake at Ann's wedding, wearing flashy diamond rings on every finger but two. We had lots of reminiscing to do.

One night they took me to the Starlight Opera to see *The Desert Song*. I fell in love with the haunting music and beautiful scenery. At the end of my visit she gave me a friendship circle, a small gold pen I fastened to my shirt collar the first day of tenth grade.

The Summer had flown by on silent wings. I signed up for first year Spanish, biology and drama class, history and English, subjects selected to further widen my horizons and get me into the college of my choice.

Little Robert took the train to college at Texas A & M, but he didn't stay long. He'd recently dedicated his life to Christ and decided to go to theology school nearer home.

He enrolled at Howard College, the Baptist College across town, planning to become a preacher. At night he studied Hebrew in our kitchen or did mission work in the poorer sections of town. Dawson's deacons ordained him to the ministry and one Sunday night my brother preached from the pulpit.

With our house emptying, Momma and Daddy had time to play closer attention to me. Though I'd craved attention all my life, I now found myself wishing for less. I moved into the attic room with the window facing the street and slept on Little Robert's narrow cot with the cozy feather mattress so I had more room for books.

Momma always slept in, but made sure she was up and dressed, usually in the red sundress Daddy liked so much when time for him to come home rolled around. Ann had made that dress with big pockets and wide straps, a fitted waist and bust. When Daddy saw her wearing it, his welcome home kiss always lasted longer, his hands plastered to Momma's firm butt.

# Chapter Eighteen

Some Men in My Life
1948-1949

In tenth grade my social horizons expanded to include Les Amies Mother-Daughter teas. Momma bought me an R & K Original to wear to mine. Gold threads running through the black taffeta fabric reflected light off what was meant to be a fitted dress. The portrait collar framed my face and I felt very grown up wearing it to social events.

When I look at photos taken then, I cringe. I looked like a ten-year-old pretending I was twenty in that too-big, too-long dress.

"Your bust will grow to fill it," Momma had assured me when I first tried on the size-ten dress, but that never happened. And my toes never stopped hurting in those patent leather pumps with ankle straps. The dress was so much too long the hem hid my shoe's straps.

Store-bought clothes swallowed me. Size ten was the smallest off-the-rack size available, so I always looked like I'd pulled my dress on too far. Dress coats intended to be knee length were full length on me and weighed me down.

I longed for clothes like Ann's. Right after graduation she'd landed a job with Southern Bell and began buying or making her own clothes, beautiful things that suited her dark coloring, petite size and height.

It didn't matter that her choice of colors and styles were not right on me. I wanted her clothes, so after she left for work, I'd sneak something from her closet, put it on, and keep my coat tightly buttoned over it so no one could see what I was wearing until I was safely on the school bus. At school, I'd stuff the coat in my locker and proudly wear Ann's sweater or skirt, pretending her clothes were mine.

My high school was u-shaped. To reach my class in the other wing I'd sometimes take the narrow path that followed the crest of a steep embankment, rather than fight my way through the crowded halls.

After a heavy rain one day, I made the mistake of cutting across wearing Ann's favorite gray wool skirt.

Down I slid on the slick red clay. When I stood, red mud covered my books, my legs, and a six-inch-wide strip of Ann's pleated skirt.

I should have come clean that night and confessed my ill-conceived deed. If I had, a trip to the cleaners might have saved the skirt, but another of my mottos was: never confess.

Never, ever own up to my mistakes.

I hid the skirt in the storage area beneath Ann's closet, hoping she'd never find it, and she didn't for months.

She yelled and fumed as expected, and of course told on me. The mud had been in there so long the cleaners couldn't get the ugly brown stain out. Ann gave me the skirt, but I wouldn't wear it either, not looking like that.

I wasn't punished. I seldom was, but I did have to give her enough of my college savings to pay for wool for another skirt.

I still longed to stand out in the crowd, and all through high school I tried to start new fashion trends. One time I even wore Little Robert's Boy Scout knickers and knee socks, hoping someone would notice me and the fad would catch on. It didn't.

Following the war, hemlines dropped so low my skirts sometimes brushed my sock tops. Most girls dressed in Gibson girl blouses or dickies under short sleeve sweaters that topped those long skirts.

In the South, college football is the main topic of conversation. If you lived in Alabama, you were either a 'Bama fan or an Auburn fan. Family members sometimes came to blows over which team was best.

On the Friday before the big game my Yankee boyfriend, Dean Shafer, could talk of nothing else. For the first time the game would be screened on closed circuit television in Birmingham's Municipal Auditorium and Dean had one of the scarce tickets for the screening.

I felt privileged when my sometimes-boyfriend, Johnny Kearney, the son of a family friend, called on Saturday morning and asked me to go to the game with him and to dinner afterwards.

He'd been a high-scoring wide receiver for Alabama until he suffered a concussion in an earlier game and almost broke his neck. He hadn't been out of the hospital long, and didn't want to go to the game alone. Most of his friends would be down on the field.

Of course, I said I'd go and hung up. *What would I wear?* was my next thought.

At that time, fans wore their Sunday best to the big game. I had nothing appropriate to wear. Juanita loaned me her stylish brown suit with wide shoulders made wider by huge shoulder pads, the latest style.

In the two-sizes-too-big suit, I must have looked like a preteen linebacker when Momma dropped me off to catch the bus. I was too busy hoping I wouldn't do anything to embarrass Johnny, like fall flat on my face in Juanita's heels, to worry about anything else.

When I stepped off the bus downtown and smiled at Johnny, I felt like I was in a dream. I was going to *the* game of the year with him.

Simply rubbing shoulders with other well-dressed fans and a date with Johnny should have satisfied me, but I kept hoping he'd buy me one of those huge chrysanthemum corsages sold on every street corner the day of the game, but he didn't offer me one.

Alabama lost by one point. Although Johnny was glum at dinner, I was basking in the afterglow from attending my first college football game. I can still see Dean Shaffer's surprised expression on Monday when I told him I had watched the sold-out game from the fifty-yard-line.

In addition to my usual class load I'd enrolled in speech and glee club that year. Dean waltzed with me in the glee club's opera, *Miss Cherry*

*Blossom*. The girls wore ankle-length gored skirts in pastel colors and ballet shoes. Janet wore yellow, I wore pink.

My cousin Mildred Ann Scott and John Tatum sang the leads. They put all their energy into the opera and poured out their love for each other on stage, which was so romantic. They hadn't noticed each other until opera tryouts, but were soon going steady, and married after graduating from college.

Right after the operetta, Janet learned her father was being transferred to Atlanta and her family was moving there.

Their December departure came all too soon and left a big hole in my life. I never had another close friend. She told me Robert Hubbard had made several trips to Atlanta on his motorcycle for weekend visits before their romance waned.

Mrs. Shirey, my speech teacher in ninth grade, had convinced me to enroll in drama. Our class put on three one act plays at a school assembly. I was stage manager for one of the plays and when we put that play on and won the weekend Drama Festival held at Montevallo College, I accumulated enough points to become a Thespian, an honorary drama society limited to serious actors who also work behind the scenes. Membership earned us a group photograph in the school annual.

It snowed so much the winter of 1949 school let out for a week. On Sunday afternoon, Dean called and invited me to his house to go sledding. Momma refused to take her car out on the slick roads. Juanita happened to be home on a weekend pass from the nursing school, so she and I walked the five miles to Dean's house and spent the afternoon taking turns sliding down the steep hill in front of his house.

On one downhill trip her sled stopped at the bottom, but Juanita kept right on going, skidding across the icy street, and scratching the fancy raised-crystal of her watch, a high school graduation gift. She was very upset. The unusual crystal was never replaced.

Dean's sled had seen plenty of prior use. He'd moved to Mountain Brook from Connecticut.

He nicknamed me Dinks, and for a while I visited the youth group at his church in Mountain Brook every other Sunday night. Then Daddy told me he thought I should support my own church, but that Dean would be welcome at ours. He only came once.

I invited him to escort me to the annual formal dance Les Amies held at Hollywood Country Club. The theme of the dance that year was *Far Away Places*. On stage, the president and her date stepped through a framed painting of palm trees, sampans and the Eiffel Tower while a live band played that song about faraway places with strange sounding names. The rest of the members then came through the opening one at a time, joined their escorts, and enjoyed the first dance. Dean, who was overly formal, fit right in.

I had to wear my orchid bridesmaid's dress, but Ann changed its look by lifting the hem of the skirt in deep swoops held in place by artificial nosegays of baby's breath. Deep rows of ruffled lace attached to the lower edge of an underskirt drew the eye when I danced. Dean presented me with a wrist corsage of cymbidium orchids. They matched my dress perfectly.

Not everything came up roses. My dog Suzie disappeared from my life but I didn't have time to grieve for her because the afternoon I first missed her Daddy brought home a squirming ball of black fur for me. Since he had always complained about Suzie's ability to produce a littler of Jim's puppies with alarming regularity, I assumed Daddy had something to do with her disappearance. I didn't question him. What Daddy said was law.

I liked the nickname Dean had given me so much I named the puppy Dinks.

Years later I learned Daddy had found Suzie dead that morning, her belly slashed. He never found out who was responsible, or why. Knowing how broken hearted I'd be, he'd found a man at work with a weaned puppy old enough to leave its mother and Daddy followed the man home after work to get a puppy for me to replace Suzie.

Dinks had markings just like Suzie, but never grew as big. She liked to tug on my rolled-up jeans. One day she missed the jeans and her sharp little teeth nicked the back of my leg. To this day I have a broken blue vessel behind my knee to remind me of her playfulness.

Then Curtis Vaughn gave me a female collie puppy and with alarming regularity large litters of puppies started arriving again.

My dogs still met the school bus every afternoon, hoping I was on it. I seldom was. I'd joined the Debater's Club and in the spring won the American Legion Essay contest. The topic was something about patriotism. My prize was a check for ten dollars and a brass medal.

I never took P.E. in high school, although I'd decided wanted to be a P.E. teacher. I was college bound, so I filled my class schedule with subjects guaranteed to get me into any college that offered me a scholarship. I loved science. The lab classes. The dissection of grasshoppers and frogs.

What I didn't enjoy was dissecting cats. The day before we were to have that lab Mr. Chamblee, our teacher, told the class he was short a few lab specimens, and if anyone knew of any homeless cats, they should bring them the next day.

Jimmy S., still a disruptive element in every class he took, brought one in. Turned out it was pregnant, but not far enough along that Mr. Chamblee could tell until the cat went under the knife. Jimmy thought it was hilarious, but our irate teacher lectured him for a week.

The tall windows of the basement classroom where Mr. Chamblee taught biology ended at street level. Beyond them cars filled a parking lot, their bumpers almost touching the school wall. Venetian blinds mounted above each window could be lowered to shut out the morning glare. By the end of school when our class met, the blinds were raised high, their cords carelessly piled on each window sill and the windows opened wide to let in the light breeze.

Every Thursday, a boy in lab left class early to go to work. On one Thursday he quietly left the room and hurried out to his car parked right outside our classroom. He started it and backed out of his parking place. As he drove away, all three of those window blinds came crashing down.

Bang! Bang! Bang!

Jimmy's delighted expression easily revealed the identity of the culprit. I'll never forget how loud Mr. Chamblee roared.

From then on, even on the hottest days, he insisted the windows stay shut.

# Chapter Nineteen

Eleventh Grade

1949-1950

All Summer, I'd looked forward to the opening of our new high school, a sprawling complex under construction for nearly two years in Mountain Brook. I would enter eleventh grade there. Shades Cahaba was to beome a junior high school.

In late August I received an invitation to join the Usherettes, a school service organization made up of the most dependable, well-behaved girls in school who earned good grades. Our first assignment involved helping students find their way around the new high school. Mrs. Hightower, our faculty advisor, anticipated a lot of confusion on the first day of school. Some of the classrooms were not finished, so temporary space for those classes had to be found and the students enrolled in those classes directed to the new location.

For the first two weeks I stood in the hall between classes and helped lost students find their way. From the outside, the modern facility composed of numerous two-story buildings, looked complete, but the driveways and parking lots were not yet paved. Thick red mud surrounded the island of buildings with no way to classes without wading through sticky red mud.

At the end of the first week the cheerleaders held a pep rally in what would someday be our new stadium. At the time it was only a shell, and the students had to cross the mud on narrow boards to reach the incomplete stands. I did my best to stir up school spirit without splattering mud on the other cheerleaders.

One day Mrs. Mackey, my English teacher, called me aside. "How would you like to write a weekly column for the Birmingham News?" she asked.

I knew right away what she meant. Once a week the local *Scripps-Howard Newspaper* published gossipy news columns written by students from each of the local high schools.

"Sure," I said, jumping at the chance.

My picture would appear in the paper every week!

She told me who to contact at the paper so I could get hired and start earning ten dollars a week for writing anything I wanted to as long as I used proper English and made sure the things I wrote were true.

My contact at the newspaper told me to drop my column in the mail on Monday so he'd have it in plenty of time to publish it on Friday. I agreed.

Before long, checks made out to me began arriving in the mail.

I endorsed them. Momma would cash them, and give Daddy the money to salt away for my college education.

He'd just grin.

Then I got a call from the editor of the *Shades Valley Sun*. "We'd like to run a weekly column of local high school news," he said, "and wondered if you'd like to write it?"

"Yes, I would." More dollar signs swam before my eyes.

"Great. Just drop your first column off at the newspaper office on Tuesday afternoon and when you come in, the staff photographer will be here to take a photograph of you to appear above your byline."

Two photographs, two bylines, twenty dollars a week. *I would soon be rich.*

Things went smoothly for about two weeks, until I began running out of ideas. I couldn't repeat the same name and cover the same events in both columns, so I had to increase my number of contacts. I learned to be careful, to not trust students known to carry grudges. Before I included an event like a party I didn't attend in someone's home, I had to verify the event really happened and confirm the names of those in attendance.

This took time, but a true writer quickly learned to write a lot about nothing, to embroidery the truth, and I became an expert at it. I wrote my column for the *Post* on Sunday night, the one for the *Sun* on Monday night. Not once in two years did I miss a deadline or take a weekend off.

The best part about being first time students in a new facility was that we were privileged to name the school paper, and the annual. The Mounties still fit, so the football team's name and mascot stayed the same.

The Science Wing was not finished so for the first two months of school, Mr. Chamblee, the teacher who taught biology, also taught my physics class. For the first two months our class met in a school bus. I was the envy of all my friends, the only girl in a class of twenty-eight. Most of the remaining class members were football players.

Many of those were brains.

After we moved into our new classroom, Mr. Chamblee began to lecture us about vision and corrective lenses.

He wore glasses with thick lenses. Rumor had it that in his youth, failing eyesight had kept Mr. C out of med school.

The lecture that day was on how the eye worked and how corrective lenses could correct the vision of those suffering from myopia and presbyopia, better known as nearsightedness and farsightedness.

No one in my family wore glasses, so I raised my hand and asked the teacher, "Which one of those conditions do you have?"

"Neither one," Mr. Chamblee replied. "Mine is an astigmatism."

Keeping a straight face, I innocently asked, "What is that? Crossed eyes?"

The room erupted in laughter. Mr. Chamblee looked like he wanted to laugh, too.

From then on I could get away with anything in his class, and frequently did.


Before Daddy let for work each morning, he'd leave two or three dollars for my lunch money and bus fare home clipped to the family message center, the metal matchbox mounted above the kitchen stove.

Most afternoons, my school bus usually ground its way down the muddy school drive without me on board, for I frequently had cheerleader practice, Les Amies meetings or donut sales, and had to miss the bus.

Les Amies members raised money year round to pay for our annual dance, so once a week we all sold donuts. In groups of three and four we'd walk to the Homewood bakery to pick up our weekly allotment, twelve bags of mouthwatering glazed donuts, a dozen to a bag.

On our way home, we'd pedaled the treats door to door wherever we thought they would sell. Of the sixty cents turned in for each bag I sold, the club treasurer kept thirty cents. Daddy always bought two dozen, so I only had to find customers for ten bags.

Once I turned sixteen, as long as I kept my grades up and was home before midnight, I could go out any night of the week, not the best idea for teenage girls.

For most students, turning sixteen meant they could drive. That was not true at our house. Momma put her foot down to any of her daughters learning to drive, and since it was Momma's car, neither Juanita nor Ann had learned to drive.

When I saw that was to be my fate, too, my stubborn, won't-take-it-lying-down persona questioned *Why not me?*

I dug in my heels and began a campaign that ended when Daddy quietly told Momma, "Sugar, it's time you let her learn to drive."

Momma wasn't happy about it, but she eventually signed the permission slip, agreeing her car insurance would cover me when I was behind the wheel.

I'd enrolled in Driver's Ed when school started, a fun class made interesting by movies and simulators to help would-be-drivers learn the rules of the road. When I finished reading the textbook I decided I was ready to drive Daddy's Model A. He drove a truck to work now, and every day left his antique Ford parked behind our house at a sharp angle to the drive.

I had watched him start that car by jiggling the gas lever mounted on the steering column to get it moving so often I was certain I knew exactly what to do.

I climbed up on the seat, shifted into Reverse and pushed the Start button on the dash.

The car flew across the drive, my head pressed back against the seat. I closed my eyes and waited for the crash.

The motor coughed once, and died. I opened my eyes to survey the damage.

It hadn't felt like I hit anything, but I was seeing only sky through the windshield. Daddy's car stopped at a really funny angle. Worse still, the front wheel on the driver's side was no longer touching the ground, and I had to slide way down out of the car before my feet reached the ground.

I walked slowly around, surveying the damage.

None, from what I could see. I got lucky, but if Daddy came home and found his car in the ditch he'd know right away what I'd been trying to do, and he'd no longer be on my side about driving.

I hurried inside and called a neighbor, and explained my fix. "Could you and your brother please come down and push Daddy's car back where it belongs before he gets home?"

They did, but had far too much fun kidding me about my driving.

Daddy's Model A was no sooner parked back where it belonged than he came rattling up the drive in his truck.

That day I dodged a bullet. No one ever found out.

My behind-the-wheel driver's training began in the Spring. I'd had the same teacher for driver's education, a lanky man not easily perturbed, so I felt comfortable around him. On the first day three students eagerly awaiting their turn to drive climbed in the back seat. The teacher handed me the keys, then folded his long legs in the passenger seat of the specially equipped car.

I took the seat behind the wheel. That's when I saw the extra set of pedals beneath my teacher's feet. "What are those for?"

"To stop the car in case of an emergency," he said, "but I've never had to use them."

Nothing ever ruffled him, former students had assured me.

Things went well the first part of the class, considering I'd never tried to shift gears or keep a car on the road before. I began feeling more sure of myself.

"Take a left on Oxmoor Road," the teacher said.

I turned out onto the busiest street in Homewood!

After a few blocks, he said, "Turn left at the next street," but failed to instruct me to slow down before making that turn.

I turned. The car headed right for the telephone pole on the corner, then suddenly stopped. The students in the backseat nearly landed in our laps. The motor died.

The driver behind me sat on his horn.

I exchanged a puzzled look with the teacher's exasperated one. "What stopped us?"

"I did, or was it your intention to hit that telephone pole? Anytime you make a turn, you need to apply the brakes."

The training car had stopped with the front bumper a bare six inches from that pole.

"It was you who slammed on the brakes?" I asked. He nodded. "Should I get out and let someone else get us out of this mess?" I meekly asked.

"No. Put the gear shift in Reverse," the teacher said calmly, "back up a little, then finish the turn."

I managed to get us out of there without further damage or incident and pulled over before the next corner so someone else could drive. One thing was certain.

I never wanted to teach Drivers Ed.

The students riding in the back seat never let me forget my first turn at the wheel.

I would never have gotten my license if Daddy hadn't put his foot down, telling Momma, "It's time," when I again refused to let the subject die. I was anxious to take my road test and I entertained visions of driving myself to school. Other students did.

*Why not me?*

It never happened, but had the need ever arisen, I could have.

Small consolation, but one time my being able to drive did help Momma out of a bind. She'd driven some Les Amies members to Panama City, Florida, for a house party over Spring Break. While there, a painful cyst came up on her privates requiring medical care. She couldn't sit, hurt too much to drive, and willingly gave me the keys. I drove her to the doctor and back without one complaint, sure proof of her pain.

Whenever someone important visited our school, we Usherettes donned uniforms of white blouses and black skirts and guided the visitors around. Since ours was a new school, the State Accreditation Committee visited our campus for an entire week.

The faculty breathed a united sigh of relief when the principal, Mr. Peake, received word the school passed accreditation and future graduates would be welcomed by the college of their choice.

As students of a new school, we enjoyed a lot of firsts. We named the annual The Tower, commemorating the two-story glass enclosure that dominated the modern entrance and housed one of the many staircases to the upper floor. The journalism class published the Valley News newspaper and Mrs. Stephens appointed me its first editor.

Mrs. Stephens entered my editorial on studiousness in an annual competition. The editorial earned my admission into Quill and Scroll, an honorary writing society. Besides writing an editorial for the Valley News published once every two weeks, I reported on the action at varsity basketball games, and my fishing column earned a byline, although I'd never been fishing in my life. Former boyfriends had, and I picked their brains.

While Momma would not hear of me driving her car, Mrs. Stephens never once questioned my driving skill. Every other week, on the day before press day, she would hand me the keys to her old Willis and send me downtown to pick up our newspaper proofs. I never let on to her how much it unnerved me to drive down Twentieth Street hill into Birmingham. If there had been another way over the mountain, I would gladly have taken it, even if it meant going out of my way.

In a special mid-year assembly, along with some of my friends, I was tapped into the National Honor Society. My failed attempt to help Jimmy S pass Mrs. Stephens' ninth grade English test had not ruined my chances to make the coveted society after all.

In the Spring I ran for student body Vice-President, convinced I would easily win. Harry P. a popular cheerleader in my homeroom also ran. He and I were in a run-off, and when all those votes were counted, he'd won. My loss ended my political aspirations and I never again ran for anything.

After elections came term paper assignments, my favorite time of year. I had a way with words and always earned an A on all written papers, but that year I turned our English assignment into a money-making scheme. With the portable typewriter Daddy bought for us I went into business.

Boys always waited until the last minute to find someone to type their paper from their note cards. For a price I offered to, but only if they completed their research well ahead of time.

I set up shop on the kitchen table and every evening, typed long after my parents had gone to bed. Daddy stashed my earnings with my college fund which had grown fat with babysitting money and those ten-dollar checks from the *Post* and the Sun for my weekly columns.

Oh. I forgot about the money I earned calling square dances for the YMCA's downtown teen canteen, Calico Corner. I called circle dances—Swing your partner. Promenade—simple calls that moved the boys around the outer circle while the girls stayed in place. Daddy taught me this call.

The YWCA was not in the best part of town, and Momma and Daddy wouldn't allow me to go there by bus, so most Friday nights they dropped me off and went to see a movie and I called square dances.

Needless to say, they were delighted that school was ending and along with it, my Friday night job.

On the last day of classes I picked up my copy of *The Tower*, the first annual of the new school, and glanced through it on the bus ride home. *Amazing.* I was in one of the photographs on nearly every page.

*Little fish in a big pond?*

Didn't look like it.

What I wouldn't have given to show my annual to Mrs. J, my teacher, mentor, and friend at Hall Kent School.

*Why not me?* I had long ago wondered, then set about proving Mrs. J wrong.

Okay. I'd achieved my goal. *Now what?*

# Chapter Twenty

Senior memories

1950-1951

In late July I rode a Greyhound bus to Milledgeville, Georgia, where I slept in a college dorm and represented my school at Girl's State.

One afternoon I walked into the small town to shop, a real novelty for me, and paid eight hard-earned dollars for a coral tee shirt. The expensive top had little puff sleeves and I wore it for the next fifteen years.

When Girl's State ended I rode the bus to Atlanta and spent a week with Janet before she and I caught a Greyhound bus to Ridgecrest, North Carolina for Training Union Week.

That was her first trip to Ridgecrest and my first time there without Momma. With no adult supervision, Janet and I got into a lot of mischief those seven days. Our roommate was a middle-aged woman. Every day, we either short-sheeted her bed or hid a slice of watermelon under her covers.

One afternoon, Janet, C.B., and I went to the railroad tracks that ran through the conference grounds and posed for some great snapshots. He was a pimply-faced boy from Church, and didn't want to be in the pictures, so I lay down on the tracks while Janet stood over me holding a big rock and while we posed he snapped several photographs with Momma's box camera. Later, with the railroad tunnel in the background, Ann was convinced she could see a train coming in one of those photographs.

The second week of school, after teaching cheerleader hopefuls a few cheers, the squad held onstage cheerleader tryouts. Every student in school received a ballot and voted for their favorites. Natalie Rosenburg and I were elected head cheerleaders and over the next three weeks we trained the newly elected team members, then kept them in line at football games.

The cars parked in the school parking lot either belonged to faculty or to boys. Few of the girls owned cars, and seldom drove a parent's car to school, and although I wasn't allowed to drive, I was finally allowed to go out on dates in cars and I did, nearly every night.

I was still riding to school on the school bus, but most days rode the city bus home because of my many after school activities.

When those various activities concluded, I caught a city bus to the end of the line and walked home. Oak Grove had undergone many changes. The streets were paved, and where cows once grazed, new houses now lined curving streets.

Some afternoons Lindel W. rode by on his motorcycle and offered to take me home. He didn't live in my neighborhood, he'd just come looking for me. We'd go for a ride first, then he'd drop me off a block from my house. Although Papa Will had ridden a motorcycle and I later learned Momma had loved to ride too, but I was not allowed to ride on one. Momma's standing rule was, "No riding on motorcycles and motorbikes."

I frequently broke that rule.

I served as President of the Usherettes, Future Teachers of America, and Thespians. Those clubs met during school.

A second year of Spanish and a year of Chemistry were the only college prerequisites left for me to satisfy.

We were required to speak only Spanish in Mrs. Morton's classroom, which I did, but my southern drawl made the Castilian Spanish she taught us unintelligible. She assigned each of us a Spanish name, and since my given name didn't translate, I became Carlotta. I thought it a very romantic name.

While my realm of knowledge was expanding, my social life was, too. Coach Mitchell put me in charge of decorations for the annual football banquet. I went all out, made standup cutouts of all the players, using photographs from the game programs and scattered them down the center of the banquet tables like testosterone-enhanced paper dolls in football uniforms. For centerpieces, I stuck gold football cutouts in vases of yellow mums. Girls weren't allowed at the banquet, but on Monday I learned the decorations were a big hit and for a week, team member spoke to me in the hall.

That fall, Johnny Kearney introduced me to one of his good friends, a Theta Chi fraternity brother at the University of Alabama. We hit it off and I went out with him every other weekend when he came to town. He invited me to Theta Chi's Holiday dance and escorted me to the Les Amies Christmas Banquet with me.

We went out one bitter cold night right before the holidays. He gave me a lovely blue silk scarf, by far the most appropriate and appreciated gift I ever received.

When the ground froze our unpaved driveway became a rutted skating rink for cars. Deep ditches lined either side and because of the icy conditions cars frequently wound up in one of the ditches paralleling the drive.

My date wisely turned in our drive and immediately stopped his car. "Mind walking from here?" he asked, then carefully walked me to my door and said goodnight.

I was heating water to go in the fruit jar that would warm my feet once I went to bed when I heard a knock on the door. "What made you come back?" I asked my crestfallen-looking date.

"I never left. My car won't start. You think your father would give me a jump?"

Poor Daddy. It was late and he was already asleep. I hated to wake him and drag him out in the cold, but he cheerfully went out to help.

While I shivered by the front door, watching, they backed the stalled car out of the drive, then pushed it far enough down the street for Daddy to drive his dependable Model A right up behind it. He pushed the other car about fifty yards down the road before it started. My toes nearly froze just watching them.

I was so busy going out with other dates I failed to notice that guy had abandoned me. Months later, Momma learned that he—and now I can't even remember his name—gave his Fraternity pin to another girl the week after Christmas, which made all his Fraternity brothers mad at him. Seems the Fraternity had overdrawn their bank account before the holidays and all members had been warned not to get pinned until the chapter was in the black. Giving a girl a Fraternity pin signified a planned engagement and tradition demanded the members send the recipient of the pin a dozen red roses, even when the Fraternity was short on funds.

In second semester Chemistry we carried out tedious and sometimes dangerous experiments in the shiny new upstairs lab. Bobby R, who'd been my lab partner for all three of my lab classes and date when needed, usually let me take the lead. We wore long rubber aprons to protect our clothing during experiments, things like testing the flammability of phosphorus and the corrosive effect of acids on metals.

One day our assignment was to make sulfuric acid in class. The teacher cautioned us to be especially careful, as someone could easily get burned.

I tightened my apron strings around my waist and read aloud the steps we would follow, which cautioned students not to pour the contents of the first beaker into the second beaker too fast.

"Ready?" I asked, ignoring a sudden sting on the back of my leg.

"Pour it nice and easy," Bobby replied.

The liquid in our beaker bubbled up slowly, giving off an acrid smell as the two chemicals mixed. B. carefully placed the beaker on a stand and I began to write up our results. That's when I realized the sting on my calf had not gone away.

I tried to look over my shoulder and see what was making my leg sting, but my head couldn't turn far enough. I asked B, "Do you see anything on the back of my leg?" and turned around for him to look.

"No, but I don't remember seeing that hole about the size of a nickel in your skirt before."

My attempts to see the damage attracted the teacher's attention. He came over and asked, "What's wrong?" It didn't take him long to figure out the careless boy working at the station behind us had poured his chemicals together too fast. The acid had spewed up and out, splashing on my leg and skirt.

If I'd connected the hole in my skirt to the stinging of my leg, I'd have told the teacher. He would have stood me in the sink for that purpose and hosed off my leg to stop the burn. As it was, I didn't connect the place on my calf to the chemistry-experiment-gone-bad until the blister began to scab over. I still have a small scar from the burn.

One February morning Mrs. Hightower, the girl's counselor, called me into her office. We'd discussed my need for a college scholarship and she'd promised to be on the lookout for one. She'd known my siblings when they were in school and was aware Daddy had again been laid off until spring.

"There's a test for a scholarship being given on Saturday that I want you to sign up for," Mrs. Hightower said, handing me an application to complete.

Early Saturday Daddy drove me to the end of the line to catch a transit bus to Philips High School, where the testing was held. When the bus stopped in Edgewood, my nemesis, Janet L, got on.

She and I started talking and soon realized we were both taking the same exam. I figured I didn't have a chance since she'd applied, too.

I'd been by Philips High School many times, but had never gone inside. The buildings were quite old, but prosperous parents who'd attended Philips continued to send their sons and daughters there.

Janet and I stepped inside. The casement windows needed a good washing. The wooden floors squeaked as we walked down the hall.

We found the crowded testing room and quietly took a seat. Then I sharpened my supply of number two pencils. I couldn't stand to write with unsharpened pencils.

Boys outnumbered the girls about two to one, but none of them had anything to say to us.

The teacher in charge read her list of instructions and the testing began. The questions seemed too easy. I kept expecting to find harder ones when I turned the next page. They never materialized. Algebra and geometry questions, history and science, and plain old problem solving kept me busy, but not one of the questions stumped me.

I was the first one through, which worried me, so I went back over my answers to make sure I hadn't skipped a question, or maybe an entire page. I couldn't find any answers that were obviously wrong or missing, so I turned in my test and caught the next bus home. Even with the three mile walk I was home by ten o'clock.

At school on Monday, Mrs. H asked how the test went.

I told her, "Unlike those standardized tests we took that measured our knowledge by ending with problems we couldn't possibly solve, Saturday's test didn't even exercise my brain."

She looked pleased.

As president of Les Amies, the honor to lead the spring dance fell on me. I invited Bobby R to escort me. We had gone out from time to time over the years, and any time I didn't have a date for some event, could depend on him to take me.

When he and I were introduced we broke through a painted paper rose while the orchestra played *To Each His Own*.

I received a dozen red roses from the members. Scarlet O'Hara would have envied the white organdy ball gown Ann had made for me. Although very pregnant, she had patiently gathered countless yards of organdy onto the tiered-and-ruffled skirt. It draped gracefully over a wide hoop that hiked up in front when I tried to sit.

Momma and Daddy were chaperones, and looked happy to be out on a dance floor again. They didn't attend the breakfast following the dance and were already in bed when Bobby took me home.

Before leaving for the dance, Momma had sewed me into the strapless gown and rather than wake her, I slept in the scratchy dress.

Soon, I was on the downhill slide to graduation. The journalism class put the last paper to bed. Before our social studies final, we picked each other's brains, trying to decide which of the current events we'd discussed in class the teacher would include on his exam.

And amidst all that confusion Mrs. Hightower called me into her office again.

"Congratulations," she said. "I just got word you scored so high on the test you took, a small college in Kentucky has offered you a full four-year scholarship."

"Test. What test?" I asked, unable to wrap my brain around her words.

"The test you took in February." Her smile widened. "You won. A small college in Kentucky has awarded you a four years college scholarship. All your expenses will be covered as long as you make good grades. Your father won't have to pay a dime. A good college education *is* within your grasp. Why don't we call your mother and tell her the good news?"

As I sat there in Mrs. H's office, waiting for Momma to answer the phone and learn my years of studying had paid off, I said a thank you prayer for Miss Hodnett, the teacher who first mentioned college and started my fertile mind wondering, *Why not me?*

The End

**Why Not Me? Is a Memoir.**

# Dedication

This book is dedicated to all my children, grand-children and great-grandchildren.

You know who you are.

**Acknowledgements**

Cover created and designed by

Carol's Cover Designs

https//www.carolscoverdesigns.com/

# Other Books by Toni Noel

Decisive Moments
Fairy Dusted
Fragile Bonds
Homeward Bound
Law Breakers and Love Makers
Lying Eyes
Restored Dreams
Rising Above
Temp to Permanent
To Feel Again
Raising Rudy Holt
Hot Soup and Cool Secrets

# Also by Toni Noel

Fairy Dusted
Lawbreakers and Love Makers
Rising Above
Lying Eyes
To Feel Again
Temp to Permanent
Fragile Bonds
Restored Dreams
Decisive Moments
Homeward Bound
Hot Soup And Cool Secrets
Hot Soup and Cool Secrets
Why Not Me?

Watch for more at www.FlameArden.com.

# About the Author

Toni Noel's romantic suspense novels are chock full of intrigue and romance. She hits the unsuspecting reader right in the heart with a hero to fall in love with as he falls in love with the heroine, whether he's an alpha detective, a reclusive architect or the tight-lipped temporary help she hires to lighten her work load. He saves her life.

Her contemporary romance novels are equally heartwarming, whether about the disenchanted CEO who hires a promising-but-inexperienced stager to prepare his Rancho Santa Fe estate for quick sale or the rodeo rider turned philanthropist a destitute teacher hires to restore her Victorian home.

Read more at www.toninoelauthor.com/books.html.